The CLASSIC TOUCH

LESSONS IN LEADERSHIP FROM HOMER TO HEMINGWAY

JOHN K. CLEMENS
AUTHOR OF *MOVIES TO MANAGE BY*
AND DOUGLAS F. MAYER

CONTEMPORARY BOOKS

Library of Congress Cataloging-In-Publication Data

Clemens, John, 1939-
    The classic touch : lessons in leadership from Homer to Hemingway
John K. Clemens and Douglas F. Mayer. — Rev. ed.
      p.   cm.
    Includes bibliographical references and index.
    ISBN 0-8092-2797-5
    1. Leadership.   I. Mayer, Douglas F.   II. Title.
HM1261.C54   1999
303.3'4—dc21   99-23272
                                         CIP

Cover design by Kim Bartko
Cover illustration copyright © William Bramhall
Interior design by Jeanette Wojtyla

Published by Contemporary Books
A division of NTC/Contemporary Publishing Group, Inc.
4255 West Touhy Avenue, Lincolnwood (Chicago), Illinois 60712-1975 U.S.A.
Printed in the United States of America
International Standard Book Number: 0-8092-2797-5
3 4 5 6 7 8 9 0   DSH/DSH   0 1 0 9 8 7 6 5

Also by John K. Clemens

Movies to Manage By
Leadership Wisdom from Great Films

(with Melora Wolff)

The Timeless Leader

(with Steve Albrecht)

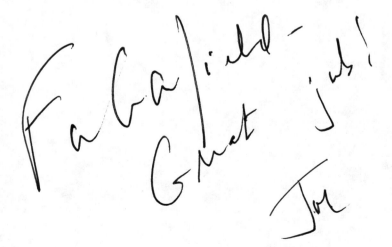

To Karyl and Susan,
who epitomize the classic touch

CONTENTS

Easy • Blow Not Thy Horn—Too Much • A Little
Humility Goes a Long Way • Pick Your Mentor Well •
Making the Boss Look Good

ACKNOWLEDGMENTS

Many people have helped make this book possible. Merrilee Gomillion, Hartwick College's former editor of publications, whose critical sense is exceeded only by her diplomatic skill, transformed countless early drafts into readable prose. Evgeniy Krasnov and Megan McConnelee served as invaluable research assistants. Anne Clemens took precious time out of her busy schedule at Digital Equipment Corporation to provide invaluable assistance throughout the two-year project.

Richard A. Detweiler, president of Hartwick College, was greatly encouraging throughout the course of the project. Jerrold C. Brown, former professor of classical languages at Hartwick, patiently checked the manuscript for accuracy. Professor Brown, political science professor Sugwon Kang, and Shakespeare professor Terrance R. Fitz-Henry, allowed one of the authors to audit their classes, an experience that was seminal to the project. Dr. Philip S. Wilder, Hartwick's former president, provided near-entrepreneurial support and critically reviewed portions of the final manuscript. Professors Thomas

Travisano and David Baldwin helped conceive the structure of the book. Peter G. Wallace, assistant professor of history, suggested the Castiglione chapter and recommended an approach to its interpretation. Art professors K. Christine Flom and Fiona Dejardin provided invaluable ideas for the book's design.

A number of corporate leaders and academicians participated in interviews that greatly increased our awareness of the powerful linkages between leadership and the ideas contained in the classics. Among them were Robert J. Higgins, president, Fleet National Bank; James March, Merrill Professor of Management, Stanford Business School; J. Terrance Murray, chairman and president, Fleet Financial Group; Guy Odom, former chairman, U.S. Home Corporation; F. G. "Buck" Rodgers, former IBM marketing vice president; Richard Rosenberg, president and CEO, Big-V Shoprite Supermarkets; and George Stephan, vice chairman, Kollmorgen Corporation.

Lee Pickett, president of Pickett Associates, and James Russo, director of government relations at SmithKline Beecham Corporation, spent many hours reviewing and improving the manuscript.

Antigoni Ladd, vice president of the Consumer Bankers Association, not only provided perceptive criticism but also helped transform the manuscript into a two-week management-training program.

Roy Rowan, a journalist who in his thirty-eight-year career has been a top editor for *Life*, a correspondent for *Time*, a member of *Fortune's* board of editors, and—most recently—author of *The Intuitive Manager*, reliably provided not only inspiration but also hard-nosed criticism. Both, as it turned out, were very necessary.

As were writing hideaways. Ted and Dana Rodman made their home on Rackliff Island, Maine, available at a moment's notice. Bob and Bessie Hersom thoughtfully sailed off to the Caribbean for a summer, leaving their Camden, Maine, home to the authors' care. Wayne and Barbara Clemens made their Lake Sunapee, New Hampshire, home available for a month— complete with two boats and unlimited research privileges at Dartmouth's Baker Library. And Blake Gardner's home in the midst of the Berkshires' apple orchards provided expansive views and unlimited inspiration.

We want to pay special tribute to our students and to the people with whom we consult. Many of the ideas presented in this book were created and confirmed during discussions with them. As an intellectual proving ground, their contribution has been incalculable.

Finally, we owe a special thanks to our editor, Matthew Carnicelli, who expressed early and enthusiastic interest in the project, encouraged us constantly, fought for us when it counted, and always, always asked for 120 percent. Our kind of leader!

Introduction

This is a practical book about leadership. It contains time-less and *time-tested* advice about how you can do a better job leading your organization, whether that organization is a fledgling entrepreneurial start-up or a Fortune 500 giant. Unlike most other books on leadership, though, it bases its advice on a unique source of wisdom. That source is the classics, those great books of history, biography, philosophy, and drama that together constitute the collective wisdom of humankind. Through them, you'll discover insights on such critical leadership tasks as team building, using power and influence, applying intuition, managing the sales force, establishing a corporate culture, delegating, and planning succession.

It's not surprising that works such as Plutarch's *Lives*, Shakespeare's *King Lear*, and Hemingway's *For Whom the Bell Tolls* offer rich perspectives on the job of leading. After all, the problems that are central to effective leadership—motivation, inspiration, sensitivity, and communication—have changed little in the past 3,000 years. These problems were faced by the Egyptians when they built the pyramids, by Alexander the Great when he created his empire, and by the Greeks when they battled the Trojans.

Leadership is a slippery and elusive concept. Even the social scientists are stumped. One researcher, after reviewing the more than 3,000 leadership books and articles that have been written over the last forty years, concludes that not much more is known about the subject now than before all the fuss began. What's more, attempts to describe successful leaders usually read more like a high school yearbook than serious research. Leaders possess, these lists airily assert, "strong desire for responsibility," "goal persistence," "self-confidence," "tolerance"—and on it goes. One study even reported that successful leaders drink a lot of coffee!

None of this gets us very far. But great literature can help, because it inevitably tells stories *in context*, stories of people dealing with people, struggling toward goals—sometimes succeeding, often failing, but constantly striving. Leading, it turns out, is much more than formulas and techniques, accounting and computers. Leaders work in a world where contradiction is commonplace, where today's right answer is tomorrow's disaster, a world in which hunch, intuition, experience, openness to untested ideas, and certainly self-assurance are more important to success than mere technical skills. The art of leading is the art of being human.

What separates great business leaders from the not-so-great often has more to do with what we call "the classic touch"—the artistry of getting others to commit themselves to their highest possible levels of achievement—than with specialized techniques. Knowledge of finance, marketing, production, and personnel is important, of course, but it often produces the kind of leader who, although able to name every single tree, may fail to notice that the forest is burning. What is needed is a broader view of leadership grounded in literature that focuses not on specialized techniques but on the vast human side of the leadership equation.

Down-to-Earth Leadership Guide

Homer's Achilles, Shakespeare's Othello, Miller's Willy Loman—these people have "been there," struggling with the same kinds of sticky, intractable, often maddening leadership problems that you face every day. You can learn from their victories—and their defeats—because the lessons learned by the authors who created these characters permeate much of what they've written. Plato's *Republic* contains more insights and lessons for leaders than any textbook. Besides being one of history's great philosophers, Plato was a down-to-earth, hands-on leader with a proven track record of successful innovation. Offended by the Sophists' approach to educating young Athenians, he didn't just ponder. He did something about it, founding an academy where lecturing was replaced by discussion and case study. It lasted more than 500 years, and its approach to teaching continues to exert a profound influence on education more than 2,500 years later. In addition, Plato did not merely *theorize* about ways to organize society; he attempted *to implement* his ideas in the city-state of Syracuse. Although in this effort he was ultimately unsuccessful, more often than not

Plato's ideas worked. He is responsible for an impressive list of breakthroughs:

- He was the first to describe and apply the benefits of what we now refer to as "managing by wandering around." Like the later peripatetic philosophers, he knew that effective leadership could not emanate from the splendid isolation of the executive suite. He took his arguments into the agora much as savvy leaders practice visible leadership today.
- He realized that leading was much more a matter of asking the right questions than of giving answers. He and Socrates invented "dialectic"—a method of questioning in order to get at the truth.
- He also realized that innovation thrives only in small, intimate settings. He limited the size of his "ideal" organization with this thought in mind.
- He recognized that entrepreneurial start-ups might require a leadership style different from that required by their successor core businesses.
- He articulated the problem of organizational stagnation and gave cogent advice about stimulating an organization's growth while slowing its decline.
- He originated the assessment center when he noted that mere credentials are no substitute for careful observation of on-the-job performance.

Clearly, there is nothing ancient about Plato's thinking; he is a kindred spirit, if not a true contemporary, of today's best leaders. Shakespeare's works, too, are packed with leadership insight. *King Lear*, for example, strikingly illustrates the folly of ill-conceived succession, sloppy decentralization, and thought-less delegation. *Macbeth* leaves us with an unforgettable sense of the high cost of intemperate ambition.

Homer's *Iliad*, dominated by the conflict between two top executives, Agememnon and Achilles, raises profound questions about leadership style, motivation, reward systems, conflict res-olution, and change. *The Odyssey*, Homer's tale of Odysseus's return from the Trojan War, is a wonderful story of a leader who overcomes all distractions in order to reach his goal.

Classic biographies reveal the successes and failures of lead-ership as no textbook can. The biographies in Plutarch's *Lives* are among the best. Written during the time of the Roman emperor Trajan (A.D. 53–117), this work chronicles the lives of notable Greeks and Romans. Packed with anecdotes, the *Lives* is an unalloyed celebration of the leader as hero. Plutarch focused on the actions of great men who directed events. His heroes decisively affected the world around them, made his-tory, and were almost without exception among the world's greatest leaders.

These great works also reflect a deep concern about a uni-versal human issue: the inherent tension between the individ-ual and the organization, between each person's desire for freedom and the organization's need to enforce order. Control-ling and resolving this tension, or at least understanding it better, is as compelling an issue in a twenty-first-century cor-poration as it was in the struggling army of Agamemnon at Troy. It is the most basic problem of leading.

The dominant thinking revealed by the literature of the classical, Renaissance, and Industrial eras helps show how humankind has attempted to deal with this tension. The ancient Greeks sought to achieve a harmonious balance between the needs of the individual and the needs of the organization. The result was a merger of private and public identities that has not been equaled since. The Renaissance exalted individual achievement and ambition, sometimes greatly changing organizations. Henry VIII, for example, disregarded organizational unity and wrenched his country from the Church in Rome. Finally, the Industrial Era brought with it a profound concern about the possible domination of the individual by the organization, a concern that was poignantly interpreted by Arthur Miller in *Death of a Salesman* and by Henry Thoreau in "Walden."

The works presented in this book are representative of these three eras and points of view. They are some of the best works in Western civilization. Taken together, they present a kaleidoscopic view of humankind—its frailties, conflicts, flaws, and wonders. Each of these works offers an indelibly rich fabric of human relationships, actions, and interactions—the fundamental materials of leadership. We have considered excerpts from these works in light of issues that leaders face every day, using *The Iliad* to reflect on motivation, *King Lear* to comment on leadership succession, *The Republic* to consider democratic leadership, and so on.

Some may criticize us for "trivializing" these great works by applying them to the everyday problems of leading. But they would be wrong. These works were created to be performed, discussed, understood, and acted upon. Leading—whether kingdoms, armies, or enterprises—has been a pervasive force throughout history. The reason the classics are so compelling is that they are about universal human problems and situations. Our premise is that the heroes of this literature mirror our own humanity, our strengths and frailties, our ability to manage. We can profit by understanding how well and how poorly they did. Considering leadership alongside the classics does not trivialize them; it enlivens them by enlightening us.

John Ruskin, a nineteenth-century English writer and social reformer, wrote that "all books are divisible into two classes: the books of the hour, and the books of all time." It is the latter category that we rely on here, because it contains some of humankind's—and leadership's—most provocative ideas. They are not new. But, in leadership as well as politics, modern practitioners do not necessarily know more about their craft than did Plato or Machiavelli. Some of the works discussed in this book doubtless are familiar to you. You will benefit, however, by reconsidering them in light of your daily life and work. You will realize that what may once have been only an obligatory academic way station can become a source of intellectual refreshment and a competitive edge in leading—that elusive quality we call "the classic touch." And just as poetry can tell a whole story and paint a full landscape with a few carefully chosen words, so can this new literature of leadership bring alive the subtle nuances of human nature and provide a richer understanding of the art of leading.

Oneonta, New York
March 1999

PART ONE

THE CLASSICAL WORLD

Searching for Management Balance

The ancient Greeks constantly questioned how they could make their society—their "organization"—work better. They searched for the "facts" of human nature and for the best methods of organizing social and political life. They looked long and steadily at man, both as an individual and in combination with others. This quest was the focus of their literature, philosophy, drama, biography, and history.

This part contains five chapters that provide insight into how the Greeks dealt with the issue of balance between individual and organization. Homer, in the eighth century B.C., made it one of the main themes of his epic poem *The Iliad*.

Describing the war between the Greeks and the Trojans, *The Iliad* focuses on the relationship between two leaders, Agamemnon and Achilles. Homer highlights their drives for personal aggrandizement and their inability to cooperate, and dramatizes the damage that their need for heroic individuality did to the organization. In *The Odyssey*, he describes—better than any modern text—the importance of avoiding distractions in order to achieve goals. Next, two excerpts from Plutarch's *Lives* show how Alexander the Great's astute assimilation policy ensured the success of his expansive merger-and-acquisition strategy and how the Roman leader Fabius saved his organization by refusing to act rashly in the face of public pressure and humiliation. Plato, in *The Republic*, takes a "second look" at democratic management, leaving us to wonder whether it is really the panacea touted by twentieth-century social scientists. *The Republic* also provides one of the best examples of Socratic dialectic—the process of question and answer—ever written, showing what an invaluable tool it is for integrating the individual and the organization, improving the ability to think critically, and enhancing communications. In his *Funeral Oration*, Pericles establishes himself as the father not only of the Golden Age of Athens but of corporate culture as well. Finally, Sophocles' play *Ajax* tells the tragic story of an individual who was unable to adapt to the changing culture of his organization. And his *Antigone* portrays a leader whose dictatorial and inflexible style of leadership destroys himself and those he loves.

Large organizations were not new. They had existed in Egypt and China for thousands of years. But the Greeks were the first to study them systematically. They were the first to ask compelling questions about organizational behavior. They wondered what effect a tyrannical leader, rather than a democratic one, might have on an organization. They were concerned about how a leader might change a decision, after it had been promulgated, without losing his authority. They explored the relationship between organizational culture and governance. They examined leadership as no people before them had ever done—how people were motivated, how they might be induced to succeed in the face of seemingly insurmountable odds. They sought to comprehend what it was that impelled diverse individuals to unite in organizations. They sought to discover how individuals could relate for the common good and mutual interest. And they were eager to discern how power and authority might best be arranged so as to preserve the two pillars of their society, freedom and respect for law.

A number of factors accounted for the Greeks' preoccupation with the individual and the organization. Certainly geography played a major role. A cursory inspection of a map of Greece shows a land crisscrossed by high mountains and deep valleys, a tortuous coastline, and numerous islands. This topography led to the development of small, autonomous, isolated communities for which self-sufficiency was an ideal. Each small town became a separate world. In addition, the simple and unostentatious lifestyle of the Greeks helped to encourage introspection and contemplation. They concentrated as much on amassing intellectual capital as they did on acquiring material wealth. They believed strongly that people possess an innate ability to apply reason to direct their destiny—that they are responsible for and in control of their lives.

Harmonizing the Individual and the Organization

These three factors—geographic isolation, a contemplative nature, and belief in reason—led the Greeks to ask history's first important questions about the nature of the relationship between individuals and organizations. Perhaps the most important factor accounting for their interest in this relationship, though, was the heroic code, which demanded that all individuals strive to achieve their fullest potential. Honor and glory, won through action, were the hoped-for results. But the heroic, individualistic values of the eighth century B.C. and earlier seemed irreconcilable with the growing needs of the organization as Greek city-states developed 300 years later. Yet, the Greeks saw that it would be destructive—and probably impossible—to eliminate individualism from their culture. They sought instead to find ways to harmonize individual and organizational demands.

The Greeks believed that balance is required to sustain the effectiveness of organizations and of the individuals in them. This meant avoiding extremes, behaving reasonably, and living moderately. Everything should be done, they thought, within limits. Balance was so important to the Greeks that Aristotle developed an entire philosophical system—the "doctrine of the golden mean"—based on it. In this system, "courage" lay somewhere between cowardice and rashness, "pride" between vanity and humility. Theoretically, Aristotle's doctrine answered these questions: How ought men, as moral beings, to behave? How can men achieve happiness? Operationally, it provided the fundamental key to the relationship between the individual and the organization, ensuring that the organization could never completely transgress the rights of the individual and that the individual could not put personal needs above those of the organization; both the individual and the organization were obliged to avoid such extremes. But, how to do it?

The Greek solution to this fractious problem was to transform society—their organization—into a mechanism in which, instead of achieving honor solely on the battlefield, every individual could become a hero by playing an important role in the organization. This meant active participation in civic affairs: attending the assembly, debating in the agora, and supporting the arts. Thus the honor and glory of individuals became closely entwined with their service to the organization. In this way, the Greeks made significant progress in reconciling the conflicting demands of individual and organization.

Nowhere was this ideal achieved more fully than in Athens during the Golden Age of Pericles. It is the subject of Pericles' *Funeral Oration*, which tells how in Athens organizational goals converged with individual goals to the benefit of both. The ideal Athens described by Pericles, however, never became a complete reality. In fact, the *Funeral Oration*, so full of optimistic promise, seemed ironic after the Peloponnesian War, for Athens was destroyed as much by the internal forces of corruption as it was by the Spartans. Factionalism, petty rivalry, political intrigue, tyranny—all played parts in bringing about Athens's demise. The Greek experience, therefore, demonstrates not only the benefits of achieving equilibrium between the needs of the individual and the needs of the organization but also the grave consequences of losing that equilibrium.

ONE

HOMER

Chronicler of Heroes

The Iliad and *The Odyssey* are the oral biographies of great leaders. These epics are not only historically accurate but also full of leadership insight. They vividly demonstrate how the chemistry between leaders can affect the success of an organization and how distractions can be managed only when goals are crystal clear.

Homer's two epics were created around the middle of the eighth century B.C. and were based on events that had occurred approximately 500 years earlier. It was businessman-turned-archaeologist Heinrich Schliemann who kindled renewed interest in Homer. Schliemann went to Turkey in 1870 to find Troy and, against all expert opinion, began excavations under a hill named Hissarlik. After a year, he made one of the most important finds in history: the remnants of the Troy described in

Homer's *Iliad*. It was just where Homer said it would be. Further evidence was found of a battle fought there at about the time reported in *The Iliad*. Six years later, in an effort to discover Agamemnon's home, Schliemann dug at Mycenae. Once again, he discovered artifacts that confirmed the reliability of Homer's works.

We know little about Homer's personal life. But we do know that he was a bard, a storyteller who performed the multiple roles of raconteur, actor, historian, news reporter, and teacher. He probably began his career by serving a lengthy apprenticeship with an established bard. He would have memorized a large repertoire of stories, learned to play a musical instrument, and mastered the art of improvisation. He probably then set out, much as actors and actresses do today, in search of a paying job. If he were talented and lucky, he would soon be performing at weddings, funerals, and celebrations of all kinds, earning his room, board, and passage in this way. On the night of a performance, he would sit at the head table, food and drink would be brought, and he would begin an evening of storytelling. If all went well, he might be held over, regaling his listeners on successive nights with tales of Greece's heroic past—always being careful, of course, to weave dramatic evidence of his host's noble genealogy into the tales.

Agamemnon and Achilles
Trouble in the Greek Executive Suite

Postmortem investigations of business disasters are rarely performed (the survivors are usually far too busy trying to pick up the pieces). But if they were performed regularly, they would reveal that business failure often has less to do with product, marketing, engineering, or financial problems than it does with the chemistry among the organization's leaders. It's the bond that exists among top managers, not just their individual talents, that determines an organization's success. When senior executives spend more time and energy in backbiting than they do in cooperating, the effect on the organization is certain to be corrosive. Other employees soon get the message, forgetting that the idea is to battle the competition, not the fellows down the hall.

The Failure to Understand Teams

Team breaking occurs with alarming frequency. The problems encountered by Union Pacific Railroad following its acquisition of Southern Pacific Rail Corp. in 1996 is a notable example. The merger creating the country's largest railroad provided more direct-rail routes between the Midwest and the West Coast which were supposed to benefit customers with faster shipping times and lower rates. The company itself expected to save more than $600 million annually. Instead, within months of the merger, the movement of freight by rail was almost at a standstill west of the Mississippi, the company couldn't tell shippers where their freight was, the railroad was being sued for millions by angry customers, and the *New York Times* called it "the most spectacular merger fiasco of modern times." The reason? Union Pacific's head honchos apparently forgot that the executive's key task is to forge a team of committed players.

Accustomed to working with the latest equipment and technology and—by their own admission—arrogant, the folks at UP clearly thought SP employees were "used to making do with chewing gum and baling wire" and had nothing to teach them about how to run a railroad. They encouraged the exodus of many SP executives and managers who were skilled at keeping the line running. Even more shortsighted, however, was their seeming lack of interest in developing a sense of teamwork with the remaining SP executives by encouraging their suggestions and advice. When UP decided the company could improve efficiency by closing a key rail yard near Houston and sorting all of its railcars at SP's large freight yard in Houston, longtime SP employees warned it wouldn't work. They knew that bringing several hundred more freight cars a day into the aging facility would overwhelm its capabilities.

Thumbing their noses at the advice, cocky UP executives went ahead with the plan. The result was unmitigated disaster that cost the railroad and its customers billions. With thirty or forty trains at a time waiting to get into Houston, blocking tracks and preventing other trains from getting through; railcars backed up as far away as California and Chicago; factories closing because they couldn't get raw materials or their products to market; and ports in California flooded with freight that ships kept delivering but the railroad couldn't pick up, UP executives were forced to admit that they had "miscalculated."[1] As one observer noted, "You take an inadequate merger plan, add Union Pacific's arrogance and its refusal to listen to the old Southern Pacific hands, and you end up with a disaster."[2]

The failure to understand the importance of team building is just as frequent as its opposite, team breaking. When Disney chairman Michael Eisner named his "best friend" Michael Ovitz as president of Walt Disney Co., the idea was for Ovitz to handle operating responsibilities for every division of the company. Ovitz, founder and "ruler" of the highly successful Creative Artists Agency, had been touted as the most powerful agent in Hollywood. Now he was eager to make his mark in the corporate world. But almost immediately, his ostentatious style and penchant for flying solo got him into trouble.

Used to being treated like a god at CAA, Ovitz didn't know how—or didn't care—to form alliances within the corporate bureaucracy. He made decisions without garnering the support of other executives. He ignored and alienated people he should have befriended. He meddled in the running of recently acquired ABC, raising the hackles of executives there. More damaging, he upset Eisner himself, who had once worked for ABC and was now intimately involved with it.

With others in the company clamoring for something to be done and Eisner's loss of faith in Ovitz came loss of any support for his efforts. His attempts to implement companywide management reforms never progressed beyond a couple of dinners between division chiefs. Other ideas he proposed were equally ignored. Not only that, Eisner did nothing to counter brutal press attacks on Ovitz prompted by angry Disney executives and others in Hollywood whom Ovitz had once intimidated. As the pressure within Disney increased for the ouster of Ovitz, he made a belated attempt at the team-building and networking efforts he had ignored previously. It was too late. Following a final meeting with Eisner, the announcement was made that Ovitz was leaving Disney.

Ultimately the problem was not about the value of Ovitz's ideas or decisions. It was about his management style, or rather his lack of it. Used to making decisions and acting on his own perceptions, Ovitz failed at Disney to seek the advice of others, to build consensus for his ideas, or apparently even to consider that there might be merit in this kind of teamwork. The irony is that it was the collective effort of other Disney executives against Ovitz that brought about his demise.[3]

THE PROBLEM AT TROY

Team breaking, it would seem, is a virulent organizational disease. But there's nothing new about this. More than 2,500 years ago, Homer told a strikingly similar tale in *The Iliad*. The story covers just a few weeks in the tenth year of the Trojan War. But it is much more than a story of a war. It is the dramatic tale of two senior managers who nearly destroy their enterprise because they cannot get along, a study of what happens when the needs of the individual and the organization are out of balance.

The major characters are Agamemnon, an arrogant and autocratic executive who was the Greeks' chief king, and Achilles, who was their best warrior. The entire Greek expeditionary force had been encamped for years outside the walls of Troy, trying valiantly to conquer this tiny town on a small hill in what is now northwestern Turkey. The situation was fast becoming intolerable: the men wanted to return home, the supply lines were overtaxed, and the costs were mounting.

In dealing with this developing crisis, Agamemnon demonstrated how little he knew about keeping the commitment and support of his greatest warrior. He cared more about proving how much greater he was than Achilles than in motivating Achilles to use his energies to solve the problem of taking Troy.

Covetous of Achilles' war prize (in those days, booty consisted partly of conquered slaves), Agamemnon announced:

> "I shall take the fair-cheeked Briseis, your prize, I myself going to your shelter, that you may learn well how much greater I am than you."

Agamemnon's possessiveness got a quick, and thoroughly negative, reaction. In history's first recorded incident of an employee grousing about not getting a fair share of the profits, Achilles responded as any disgruntled employee might:

> "And now my prize you threaten in person to strip from me, for whom I labored much, the gift of the sons of the [Greeks]. Never, when the [Greeks] sack some well-founded citadel of the Trojans, do I have a prize that is equal to your prize. Always the greater part of the painful fighting is the work of my hands; but when the time comes to distribute the booty, yours is far the greater reward, and I with some small thing yet dear to me go back to my ships when I am weary with fighting."

As a team builder, Agamemnon turned out to be a dismal failure. In taking Achilles' war prize, Agamemnon robbed him of his most important symbol of power. Achilles then did what many managers would do under similar circumstances. He refused to fight. He moved his battalions out. He considered going to work for the competition, the Trojans. Injuring

Achilles' pride had catastrophic consequences for the Greeks: the loss of many lives.

The lesson is unforgettable. When top managers fail to form a cohesive team, the results can be disastrous. In the case of the Greeks, they lost a battle, and almost lost the war.

To Agamemnon's credit, it didn't take him long to mend his ways. Soon after Achilles and his men left the Greek army to fend for itself, Agamemnon tried to entice Achilles back:

> "I am willing to make all good, and give back gifts in abundance. Before you all I will count off my gifts in their splendor: seven unfired tripods; ten talents' weight of gold; twenty shining cauldrons; and twelve horses, strong, race-competitors who have won prizes in the speed of their feet. . . . I will give him seven women of Lesbos . . . and with them shall go the one I took from him, the daughter of Briseus. . . . I will honor him with Orestes, my growing son. . . . I will grant to him seven citadels. . . . All this I will bring to pass for him, if he changes his anger."

It didn't work. Achilles' response proved that a turned-on employee is a blessing money can't buy:

> "I hate his gifts. I hold him light as the strip of a splinter. Not if he gave me ten times as much, and twenty times over as he possesses now, not if more should come to him from elsewhere, or gave all that is brought in to . . . Thebes of Egypt, where the greatest possessions lie up in the houses, . . . not if he gave me gifts as many

as the sand or the dust is, not even so would Agamemnon have his way with my spirit until he had made good to me all this heartrending insolence."

KILLING THE MESSENGER

Achilles was not the only individual affected by Agamemnon's wrongheaded leadership style. When the war turned against the Greeks, Achilles sought advice from the prophet Kalchas. Kalchas was so afraid of Agamemnon that he would help only if promised protection:

> "You have bidden me, Achilles . . . to explain to you this anger of Apollo the lord who strikes from afar. Then I will speak; yet make me a promise and swear before me readily by word and work of your hands to defend me, since I believe I shall make a man angry who holds great kingship. . . . For a king when he is angry with a man beneath him is too strong, and suppose even for the day itself he swallow down his anger, he still keeps bitterness that remains until its fulfillment deep in his chest. Speak forth then, tell me if you will protect me."

Kalchas may have been promised protection from physical harm, but he suffered the lesser fate of messengers of bad news, both ancient and modern—the boss's wrath. Absent the Homeric melodrama, we've all seen bosses who act like this:

> Among them stood up . . . Agamemnon raging, the heart within filled black to the brim with anger from

beneath, but his two eyes showed like fire in their blaz-
ing. First of all he eyed Kalchas bitterly and spoke to
him: "Seer of evil: never yet have you told me a good
thing. Always the evil things are dear to your heart to
prophesy, but nothing excellent have you said nor ever
accomplished."

This would not have happened at German computer-maker
Siemens Nixdorf Informationssysteme, where dramatic restructuring of the company by chief executive Gerhard Schulmeyer
has made teamwork and employee entrepreneurial behavior the
norm. Recruited to turn around the failing company, Schulmeyer immediately compressed a rigid, seven-layer hierarchy
and installed younger managers, some lured from rival companies. More critical to the company's successful turnaround,
however, were four weeklong corporate retreats designed to
strike at the heart of traditional German management culture.
The idea was to promote the development of a new corporate
culture that invited employees to play an intimate role in determining the company's future.

Schulmeyer's insistence that everyone be on a first-name
basis was just the beginning. Employees participated in sessions
to promote team building, problem solving, improvisation, and
personal initiative. They heard firsthand complaints from
customers and distributors, intended, said Schulmeyer, "to shat-
ter complacency." At the final retreat, entrepreneurial teams of
twenty employees were asked to devise plans to improve
productivity.

The result? Higher production rates, along with effective
cost-cutting measures, enabled the company to begin compet-

ing successfully in the PC market. The bottom line showed a profit after several years of red ink. Managers and workers alike have learned that Schulmeyer values their ideas. He told employees that in the past, "managers with the most years of experience were rated the best" but "that's wrong." There might be someone else, he said "even a sixteen-year-old," with a better idea. And ideas are what he's looking for. By encouraging his employees, at every level in the company, to think like entrepreneurs instead of corporate drones, he has transformed a staid bureaucracy into a laboratory for testing innovative management tools. More important, by making his employees a valued resource within the company, he has increased the value of the company as well.[4]

Schulmeyer seems to be on to something that Agamemnon—and both the folks at Union Pacific and Ovitz—failed to see. They apparently thought that the most important thing was to show how powerful they were, hoping that this would solidify their leadership. They lost sight of the leader's most important job: inspiring the team toward the attainment of the organization's objectives.

Odysseus
Demolishing Distractions and Stretching Resources

"Nothing succeeds like success," said Alexandre Dumas, the nineteenth-century French novelist and playwright. He was right, of course. In the demanding calculus of leadership, it's not enough just to do "your best." Like it or not, Vince Lombardi's purported dictum that "winning isn't everything, it's the only thing" seems to be as applicable in the boardroom as on the playing field. And winning anywhere, it turns out, depends on one thing: an almost slavish dedication to a well-defined goal. Look closely at the anatomy of successful leadership, and you'll generally see a near-monomaniacal leader in hot pursuit of an almost palpable objective.

GOALS AND GOLF

There is magic here, something inexplicable but immensely powerful. To help explain how goals work, William Mobley, who researches organizational behavior at the University of South Carolina, considered the game of golf. Why are so many people motivated to play this game that requires you to hit a little white ball around a field? What specific characteristics does the game possess? Besides the superficial "I enjoy the exercise," there is something more, observed Mobley. "One of the most important things about the game of golf," he concluded, "is the presence of clear goals. You see the pins, you know the par—it's neither too easy nor unattainable, you know your typical score, and there are competitive goals—competitive with par, with yourself, and with others. These goals give you something to shoot at, literally and figuratively. In work, as in golf, goals motivate excellence and success in the game."[5]

THE PROBLEM WITH MBO

Goal-oriented management behavior has been labeled "management by objectives" by Peter Drucker, whose astute observations on leadership have become something of a bible. "MBO," as it is known by savants, has become one of the most popular management techniques used in industry. Like most other management theories, it is disarmingly straightforward. Top management sets overall strategic goals for the organization. Then subordinates set their goals and are given a great deal of autonomy on how to achieve them. Potential chaos is transformed into a finely tuned machine by the simple mechanism of frequent performance appraisals.

Things are not so simple. For myriad reasons, MBO has failed more times than it has worked. In a recent survey of Fortune 500 companies, less than 10 percent of respondents found the technique "highly successful." For some, failure came because the organization was quickly buried under the mountain of paperwork that its MBO system generated. For others, the cause of failure was the highly structured review process, which sometimes seemed almost childish. But for most, MBO's downfall was caused by something more insidious: the inability to manage distractions, those pesky and ubiquitous events that steal a leader's attention. A phone call came just at the moment a plan was being crystallized. A meeting intruded on the completion of a project. The day's schedule was disrupted by the need to drive across town to handle an emergency at the plant.[6]

No classic better dramatizes the potentially destructive power of distractions than Homer's *Odyssey*. This epic, one of the most popular stories in Western culture, tells of how Odysseus, at the end of the Trojan War, returned from Troy to his home in Ithaca. Even for the crafty Odysseus, who had devised the Trojan horse to sneak Greeks into Troy, it was not an easy journey. He lost his fleet of ships. All of his companions died. Even Poseidon, the Greek god of the sea, was against him. The trip, beset by delays, errors, whims of the gods, foul weather, seduction by women, and the willfulness of his shipmates, took ten years. And when he finally got home, Odysseus had the ugly problem of facing a large gang of his wife's rowdy suitors.

A VERY MODERN DISTRACTION

What makes *The Odyssey* so relevant for modern leaders is the agility with which Odysseus regularly overcame some monumental distractions. The first occurred when he and his men reached the land of an indolent, dreamy, and forgetful people called the lotus-eaters. Odysseus told the story at a banquet held in his honor:

> "On the tenth day we landed in the country of the lotus-eaters, who live on a flowering food, and there we set foot on the mainland, and fetched water, and my companions soon took their supper there by the fast ships. But after we had tasted of food and drink, then I sent some of my companions ahead, telling them to find out what men, eaters of bread, might live here in this country. I chose two men, and sent a third with them, as a herald. My men went on and presently met the lotus-eaters, nor did these lotus-eaters have any thoughts of destroying our companions, but they only gave them lotus to taste of. But any of them who ate the honey-

sweet fruit of lotus was unwilling to take any message back, or to go away, but they wanted to stay there with the lotus-eating people, feeding on lotus, and forget the way home. I myself took these men back weeping, by force, to where the ships were, and put them aboard under the rowing benches and tied them fast, then gave the order to the rest of my eager companions to embark on the ships in haste, for fear someone else might taste of the lotus and forget the way home, and the men quickly went aboard and sat to the oarlocks, and sitting well in order dashed the oars in the gray sea."

Odysseus and his men had been blown far to the south by one of the treacherous "meltemi" winds that plague the Mediterranean Sea. Some scholars believe that they landed on an island now known as Djerba, off the coast of Tunisia. But what about the lotus flower? It does not exist, nor has it ever, on Djerba. A more likely guess is that Odysseus was faced with the same distracting problem that many leaders must deal with today: his men were very possibly getting high on hashish. But Odysseus's goal was to get home, not to provide drug counseling. Without delay, he sailed away.

ANCIENT DISTRACTIONS

The distractions of Djerba were minor compared with what was to come. Arriving at an unknown location—probably near Naples, Capri, or Crete—Odysseus and his men found themselves in the midst of a race of subhuman cannibals, the Cyclops. Leaving most of his group in a protected cove, Odysseus went ashore with a party of twelve men. It soon became an expedition that they were all to regret:

> "But when the young Dawn showed again with her rosy fingers, we made a tour about the island, admiring everything there, and the nymphs, daughters of Zeus of the aegis, started the hill-roving goats our way for my companions to feast on. At once we went and took from the ships curved bows and javelins with long sockets, and arranging ourselves in three divisions cast about, and the god granted us the game we longed for. . . .
>
> "Lightly we made our way to the cave, but we did not find him [the Cyclops] there; he was off herding on the range with his fat flocks. We went inside the cave and admired everything inside it. Baskets were there, heavy with cheeses, and the pens crowded with lambs and kids. They had all been divided into separate groups, the firstlings in one place, and then the middle ones, the babies again by themselves. And all his vessels, milk pails, and pans, that he used for milking into, were running over with whey. From the start my companions spoke to me and begged me to take some of the cheeses, come back again, and the next time to drive the lambs and the kids from their pens, and get back quickly to the ship again, and go sailing off across the salt water; but I would not listen to them—it would have been better their way—not until I could see him, see if he would

give me presents. My friends were to find the sight of him in no way lovely."

The decision to stay in the cave was one of the worst management decisions Odysseus ever made:

> "[The cruel monster] sprang up and reached for my companions, caught up two together and slapped them, like killing puppies, against the ground, and the brains ran all over the floor, soaking the ground. Then he cut them up limb by limb and got supper ready, and like a lion reared in the hills, without leaving anything, ate them, entrails, flesh, and the marrowy bones alike. We cried out aloud and held our hands up to Zeus, seeing the cruelty of what he did, but our hearts were helpless."

The next day was no better. The Cyclops hungrily consumed two more men, then promised to devour the rest in short order. Following his custom of sealing the entrance to the cave with a large boulder upon entering or leaving, he took his flocks to the field.

With his usual enterprise, Odysseus averted even this potential catastrophe. Realizing that if they killed the giant as he slept, they would be imprisoned in the sealed cave, Odysseus and his men devised a plan. They got the Cyclops drunk when he returned that evening. Before he passed out, the giant insisted on knowing Odysseus's name, and the crafty warrior answered, "Nobody." Then, while the Cyclops was in a deep sleep, the men blinded him. When his neighbors responded to

his screams and were told that "Nobody" was responsible, they
wandered off. The next morning, when the Cyclops removed
the boulder to allow his livestock to graze, the Greeks escaped
by clinging to the bellies of the sheep.

THE ULTIMATE OFFICE DISTRACTIONS

But Odysseus wasn't home yet. He and his men were forced to
pass the island of the Sirens, a race of alluring women whose
beautiful singing attracted unwary mariners onto the rocks.
Whether caused by whistling gusts of air, wind in the rigging,
or the allure of the Mediterranean, the Sirens' song was a for-
midable challenge. To overcome it, Odysseus plugged his crew's
ears with wax and had himself lashed to the mast so that he
could not leap overboard while he listened. His strategy
worked, and the ship sailed safely past.

Then Odysseus faced a classic management decision. He
had to choose between two routes, both of them thoroughly
unappealing. They were described to him by the goddess Circe:

> " 'Then, for the time when your companions have driven
> you past [the Sirens], for that time I will no longer
> tell you in detail which way of the two your course must
> lie, but you yourself must consider this in your own
> mind. I will tell you the two ways of it. On one side
> there are overhanging rocks, and against them crashes
> the heavy swell of dark-eyed Amphitrite. The blessed
> gods call these rocks the Rovers. By this way not even
> any flying thing, not even the tremulous doves, which

carry ambrosia to Zeus the father, can pass through. . . .
No ship of men that came here ever has fled through,
but the waves of the sea and storms of ravening fire
carry away together the ship's timbers and the men's
bodies. . . .

   " '. . . of the two rocks, one reaches up into the wide
heaven with a pointed peak, and a dark cloud stands
always around it. . . . Halfway up the cliff there is a cave,
misty-looking . . . from the hollow ship no vigorous
young man with a bow could shoot to the hole in the
cliffside. In that cavern Scylla lives, whose howling is
terror. Her voice indeed is only as loud as a newborn
puppy could make, but she herself is an evil monster. No
one, not even a god encountering her, could be glad at
that sight. She has twelve feet, and all of them wave in
the air. She has six necks upon her, grown to great
length, and upon each neck there is a horrible head, with
teeth in it, set in three rows close together and stiff, full
of black death. Her body from the waist down is holed
up inside the hollow cavern, but she holds her heads
poked out and away from the terrible hollow. . . . never
can sailors boast aloud that their ship has passed her
without any loss of men, for with each of her heads she
snatches one man away and carries him off from the
dark-prowed vessel.

   " 'The other cliff is lower; you will see it, Odysseus,
for they lie close together. You could even cast with an
arrow across. There is a great fig tree grows there, dense
with foliage, and under this shining Charybdis sucks

down the black water. For three times a day she flows it
up, and three times she sucks it terribly down; may you
not be there when she sucks down water, for not even
the Earthshaker could rescue you out of that evil.' "

Odysseus chose the lesser of two evils as he passed between
the monster Scylla and the whirlpool Charybdis, through a narrow strait that classical geographers have located in the Strait of
Messina between Italy and Sicily. Concealing from his men that
they could not hope to pass through the strait without loss of
life, he headed for Scylla. He chose to sacrifice some of his men
to the monster rather than lose them all to the whirlpool, and
as predicted, six men were lost. Like many leaders faced with a
no-win situation, Odysseus could only hope to cut his losses.
He describes the horror of the experience:

"So we sailed up the narrow strait lamenting. On one
side was Scylla, and on the other side was shining
Charybdis, who made her terrible ebb and flow of the
sea's water. When she vomited up, like a caldron over a
strong fire, the whole sea would boil up in turbulence,
and the foam flying spattered the pinnacles of the rocks
in either direction; but when in turn again she sucked
down the sea's salt water, the turbulence showed all the
inner sea, and the rock around it groaned terribly, and
the ground showed the sea's bottom, black with sand;
and green fear seized upon my companions. We in fear
of destruction kept our eyes on Charybdis, but meanwhile Scylla out of the hollow vessel snatched six of my
companions, the best of them for strength and hands'

work, and when I turned to look at the ship, with my other companions, I saw their feet and hands from below, already lifted high above me, and they cried out to me and called me by name, the last time they ever did it, in heart's sorrow. And as a fisherman with a very long rod, on a jutting rock, will cast his treacherous bait for the little fishes . . . then hauls them up and throws them on the dry land, gasping and struggling, so they gasped and struggled as they were hoisted up the cliff. Right in her doorway she ate them up. They were screaming and reaching out their hands to me in this horrid encounter. That was the most pitiful scene that these eyes have looked on in my sufferings as I explored the routes over the water."

But Odysseus conquered the narrow strait, just as he conquered all of the other distractions that deterred many lesser mortals—predatory monsters, narcotic flowers, an angry sea, dangerous witches, and seductive nymphs. And, although it took ten years and he was the last of the Greeks to return from the Trojan War, he *did* finally return home to Ithaca and his wife Penelope and their son Telemachus.

STRETCHING RESOURCES

Odysseus's strength lay in his resourcefulness. He knew how to augment his rapidly dwindling resources by forging informal linkages to other people across organizational lines. He boot-legged, persuaded, threatened, cajoled, and even begged. He knew that scarce resources are more frequently allocated on the basis of the squeaky-wheel principle than on the basis of any elegant, formalized system. Lesser men would not have been able to persuade Aeolus, the king of the winds, to provide sail-power for the trip home in the form of the famous "bag of winds." And no leader who stood purely on "organizational form" could have won Circe's favor and support.

Although organization charts suggest clear distinctions about who does what with which and to whom, in reality every organization is a loose confederacy of individuals—as motley a group as Odysseus ever met. What appears to be orderly and predictable on paper is, in reality, incredibly messy and grandly changeable. Dotted-line relationships, informal coalitions, and ad hoc alliances—not formalized boxes connected by vertical and horizontal lines—are pervasive in even the most militaristic and bureaucratic organization. Consequently, the leader who relies too heavily on formalized organization structure (the organization as it is "supposed to be") will surely fail to get the maximum out of the available resources. A colleague more willing to tolerate ambiguity and uncertainty may, like Odysseus, look a bit sloppy but will inevitably fare better. The former has an idealized (and highly inaccurate) perception of how organizations work; the latter's operating instincts are grounded in fact.

DEMOLISHING DISTRACTIONS

Finally, Odysseus was successful because—having marshaled his resources—he rarely lost sight of his goal. He made management by objectives work because he was obsessed with the idea of getting home, and this sustained him for ten years. Because of this, he became that rare individual mentioned earlier, the monomaniac with a mission who outmaneuvers even the most alluring distractions.

Finding a modern Odysseus is no easy task, but one leader comes to mind. He is C. Michael Armstrong, a man described as "fierce" in his dedication to eliminating those things that deter a company from its appointed mission. As former CEO of Hughes Electronics, for example, he jettisoned the company's defense holdings, chopped away the fat, and made the automotive electronics supplier lean and competitive. So, when he was tapped for the top position at AT&T, a company characterized as bloated, sluggish, and boring, telecom watchers sat up and took notice.

Things began to change quickly with Armstrong as CEO. Within a few months of taking over at AT&T, he refocused the company on its core business of telecommunications by divesting it of its credit card and communications outsourcing units. To help move AT&T back into the lucrative local market, he acquired highly sought-after Teleport, a local exchange carrier with networks in sixty-five cities. This move, applauded even by the competition, gave AT&T local access without the expense of building its own networks. The outcome was the ability to offer long-distance and local service in a single package to high-end business customers.

Next Armstrong set about dismantling other roadblocks to increased earnings and larger market share. Buyouts and layoffs reduced overstaffing and helped pare annual expenses. Salaries for top management became linked closely with performance.

Planning was instituted on how to move the company into the lead in bundling communication services in one package for customers.

Investors reacted positively to Armstrong's bold moves and dedication to transforming AT&T into the preferred carrier nationwide. Share prices began to rise steadily. So did AT&T's prestige, as increased profits and the best operating margin in the industry brought a new sense of energy and excitement to the company that some had written off as a has-been.

Armstrong's formula for the turnaround is simple: "The situation demanded a degree of intensity and focus on the challenges, assessing the alternatives and coming up with a direction."[7] And like Odysseus, once that direction was determined, he knew how to keep his eye on the goal and distractions at bay.

Like Odysseus's journey, the path of leadership is often arduous. Along the way, commitment to the goal, resourcefulness in achieving it, and the ability to overcome distractions are all-important. Whether the goal is returning home after ten years, achieving a sales objective, increasing earnings per share, or bringing about a productivity improvement, it is the "Odyssean" focus that gets results.

TWO

PLUTARCH

Biographer of Great Leaders

For anyone who wants to know what makes leaders tick, Plutarch's *Lives* is must reading. His biography of Alexander the Great, for example, offers rich insight into the mind of one of history's greatest merger-and-acquisition specialists. And his biography of Fabius describes why the Roman consul made the tough decision to delay, rather than rushing to attack, when Hannibal's army was massed outside Rome. Sometimes, it turns out, the best decision is the decision to delay, even when that decision may mean giving up personal prestige and honor.

Plutarch was a Greek who lived during a time when the Romans occupied much of his country. Not surprisingly, much of the *Lives* is his thinly veiled attempt to prove Greek leaders as capable as their Roman counterparts. Plutarch does this by comparing one against the other in a series of twenty-two parallel biographies. His subjects are notable Greeks and Romans, such as Julius Caesar, Pompey, Pericles, and Alexander. The *Lives* is full of "inside" stories about great leaders. Plutarch was interested not only in reporting mere facts but also in entertaining and edifying, aims that many modern historians and biographers find disturbingly "unprofessional." Even so, most of them would agree that Plutarch contributed greatly to the development of a new literary genre: a kind of discourse that relied less on the great events that historians prefer and more on the highly readable and engaging human minutiae of which good biography consists. Plutarch had a keen sense of the subtle differences between biography and history:

> The multitude of . . . great actions affords so large a field that I were to blame if I should not by way of apology forewarn my reader that I have chosen rather to epitomize the most celebrated parts of their story, than to insist at large on every particular circumstance of it. It must be borne in mind that my design is not to write histories, but lives. And the most glorious exploits do not always furnish us with the clearest discoveries of virtue or vice in men; sometimes a matter of less moment, an expression or a jest, informs us better of their characters and inclinations, than the most famous sieges, the greatest armaments, or the bloodiest battles whatsoever.
>
> Therefore, as portrait painters are more exact in the lines and features of the face, in which the character is seen, than in the other parts of the body, so I must be

allowed to give my more particular attention to the marks and indications of the souls of men, and while I endeavour by these to portray their lives, may be free to leave more weighty matters and great battles to be treated by others.

Alexander the Great
Blending Different Organizations

Many acquisitions and mergers do not work out as planned. Many never live up to the expectations of the acquiring company. Some break up completely. A review of these broken corporate marriages reveals that things rarely go wrong because of marketing, production, or finance. More typically, they go wrong because of a kind of myopia: the acquiring firm's leaders fail to notice how different the two organizations are. One organization may be research driven, the other marketing driven; or one may be inflexible and bureaucratic, the other informal and spontaneous; or one may be risk averse, the other eager to roll the dice. Even when there's a near-perfect match, acrimony between partners in an arranged corporate marriage can doom the marriage to failure.

One has only to look at the problems that beset Cendant, the Fortune 500 company created in 1997 by the merger of hotel and real estate franchiser HFS and direct marketer CUC, to realize how quickly a marriage between equals can disintegrate. Although HFS's Henry Silverman and CUC's Walter Forbes agreed to equally share power in running Cendant, any sense of

loyalty toward the other was lost when HFS executives charged
CUC with inaccurate reporting of its financial condition before
the merger. As a result, Silverman wanted Forbes to cede control of the company; Forbes said he'd done nothing wrong and
wasn't leaving. The bitterness that erupted between the two
had senior managers taking sides, Cendant's board in turmoil,
and neither executive speaking to the other—hardly a marriage
made in heaven.[1]

CORPORATE DIVORCE COURT

The inability of corporate marriage partners to assimilate different operating styles into a cohesive entity leads to many
failed mergers. So does failure to acknowledge each partner's
strengths and devise a plan to rule together accordingly. Add to
the mix the unwillingness of some partners to consider sharing
power, and the result may be a marriage that's over before it
begins. That was the reputed reason why the proposed merger
in 1998 between pharmaceutical giants Glaxo Wellcome and
SmithKline Beecham never took place. Initially, Glaxo's chairman, Sir Richard Sykes, had agreed he would be chairman of
the new firm; SmithKline's chief, Jan Leschly, would be CEO;
and Leschly's second-in-command, Jean-Pierre Garnier, his des-
ignated successor. But with Sykes based in London and Leschly
and Garnier in Philadelphia, Sykes became concerned that the
real power in the prescription-drugs business would be in the
United States and his own executive power would be dimin-
ished. The $70 billion merger, which would have made it the
world's largest corporate marriage, was called off, with each side

blaming the other for their failure to make it to the altar. SmithKline accused Sykes of changing his mind about who was to fill key executive jobs and trying to change a merger of equals into a takeover. Glaxo accused SmithKline of attempting a power grab with its intention of running the merged firm from its base in the United States.

Strategically, the merger had made sense for both companies. SmithKline would have received help in developing its possible drug targets, while Glaxo could have benefited from SmithKline's genetic technology. Unfortunately, the benefits of working together were overshadowed by egotistical concerns about who was going to rule over whom.[2]

MERGER-ACQUISITION EXPERT IN THE MAKING

Had Glaxo executives been better versed in the classics, they might have known that a better way to manage mergers was perfected by Alexander the Great more than 2,000 years ago. Alexander's life was promising from the start. His mother claimed descent from Achilles, which may explain Alexander's lifelong fascination with Homer's *Iliad* (he carried a copy of it through all his campaigns). His father was Philip, king of Macedonia, who had the good sense to have his son tutored by the philosopher Aristotle.

The stories about Alexander's youth leave no doubt that here was a king in the making. When asked as a boy whether he would run a race in the Olympic Games, he replied that he would, if he "might have kings to run with." And when his father's best trainers failed to tame a huge horse, Alexander succeeded, having noticed that the horse was merely frightened by its shadow. At this, Alexander's chagrined father said, "My son, Macedonia is too small for you; seek out a larger empire worthier of you."

Of course, he did just that. Alexander, it turns out, had all the savvy of a twentieth-century corporate climber:

> While he was yet very young, he entertained the ambassadors from the king of Persia, in the absence of his father, and entering much into conversation with them, gained so much upon them by his affability, and the questions he asked them, which were far from being childish or trifling (for he inquired of them the length of the ways, the nature of the road into inner Asia, the character of their king, how he carried himself to his enemies, and what forces he was able to bring into the field), that they were struck with admiration of him, and looked upon the ability so much famed of Philip [his father] to be nothing in comparison with the forwardness and high purpose that appeared thus early in his son.

But there was a darker side. Alexander brooded that his boss's successes might diminish his own importance:

> Whenever he heard that Philip had taken any town of importance, or won any signal victory, instead of rejoicing at it altogether, he would tell his companions that his father would anticipate everything, and leave him and

them no opportunities of performing great and illustrious actions. For being more bent upon action and glory than either upon pleasure or riches, he esteemed all that he should receive from his father as a diminution and prevention of his own future achievements; and would have chosen rather to succeed to a kingdom involved in troubles and wars, which would have afforded him frequent exercise of his courage, and a large field of honor, than to one already flourishing and settled, where his inheritance would be an inactive life, and the mere enjoyment of wealth and luxury.

An Astute Assimilation Policy

Alexander's organization was far from inactive. On his father's death in 336 B.C., Alexander succeeded to the throne and immediately executed all real and imagined rivals. That year, he was acclaimed as "invincible" by the Delphic priestess. In 334, he began his expedition against Persia, motivated by the need for its wealth. He was a fine planner, departing Macedonia with not just an army but also with surveyors, engineers, architects, scientists, court officials, and historians.

He first visited Troy, where he paid a tribute to Homer, whose *Iliad* he was reported to read every evening. He then conquered Asia Minor. At Gordium, he cut the Gordian knot, which by tradition could be loosed only by the man who was to rule all of Asia. By 332, he had traveled to the Mediterranean coast, where he stormed Tyre. He was welcomed as a deliverer in Egypt, whose leaders quickly surrendered. Here he founded the city of Alexandria. In 331, he took Babylon and was declared "lord of Asia." By 327, he had projected his power deep into India.

In less than ten years, Alexander had become the ruler of half the known world. He managed to hold his empire together less by force than by an astute policy of assimilation. Newly acquired Persian territories were not told to "fall in line" but instead were encouraged to retain their local administrative structure and culture. Aristotle had taught Alexander to think only of Greeks as free men and of all others as slaves. But Alexander disagreed. He admired the Persians' organizational ability, and instead of ruling over them, he decided to rule with them. He insisted that his leaders adopt local customs. In wearing native clothing, the boss set the example:

> He marched into Parthia (an ancient country southeast of the Caspian Sea), where not having much to do, he first put on the barbaric dress, perhaps with the view of making the work of civilizing them the easier, as nothing gains more upon men than a conformity to their fashions and customs.

At first he wore this habit only when he conversed with the barbarians, or within doors, among his intimate friends and companions, but afterward he appeared in it abroad, when he rode out, and at public audiences.

Appropriate clothing was only part of it. Alexander recognized the importance of blending different cultures together. He knew that goodwill was a stronger strategy than compulsion. Alexander and his army adopted many Persian customs. As Plutarch noted:

> He more and more accommodated himself in his way of living to that of the natives, and tried to bring them also as near as he could to the Macedonian customs, wisely considering that while he was engaged in an expedition that would carry him far from thence, it would be wiser to depend upon the goodwill that might arise from intermixture and association as a means of maintaining tranquility, than upon force and compulsion.

Then he made the ultimate merger commitment. He married the other CEO's daughter:

> His marriage with Roxana, whose youthfulness and beauty had charmed him at a drinking entertainment, where he first happened to see her taking part in a dance, . . . was indeed a love affair, yet it seemed at the same time to be conducive to the object in hand. For it gratified the conquered people to see him choose a wife from among themselves, and it made them feel the most lively affection for him, to find that in the only passion that he, the most temperate of men, was overcome by, he yet forebore that he could obtain her in a lawful and honorable way.

Alexander allowed local leaders to continue governing. When the eldest leader of a conquered small province in India fearfully asked what he and his countrymen might do to earn Alexander's friendship, Alexander replied, "I would have them choose you to govern them." He knew how to bring a newly acquired manager into the fold.

Alexander's enlightened strategy for acquisitions and mergers meant that his new territories could maintain that which was dearest to them: their separate culture and identity. Fusing disparate organizational cultures is just as important today as it was 2,000 years ago. Doing this in a merger is far more important, and usually much more difficult, than consolidating financial statements and combining plants.

The merger of Upjohn Co. in the United States and Sweden's Pharmacia AB in 1995 to create Pharmacia & Upjohn Inc. is a good example. The linkup was supposed to help both pharmaceutical companies' aging product lines and improve their ability to compete with drug giants. But merging their vastly different cultures proved to be a gargantuan task, one further complicated by the fact that Pharmacia also had operations in Italy. The Americans' aggressive, direct, and in-your-face management style was offensive to the Europeans. The Swedes, used to working in autonomous teams and having a say in major decisions, were nonplussed by demands that they submit frequent detailed reports on research, budget updates, staffing changes, and travel plans. They also bristled at Upjohn's random drug and alcohol testing of workers and its ban on smoking. The Americans grumbled about their objections. The Italians, insulted by Upjohn managers who constantly asked for verification of data, and afraid they would lose their voice in the company, complained vociferously about the American "takeover." At the same time, the Americans and Swedes saw the Italians' custom of leaving work to take care of a child or sick relative as a lack of company loyalty. Meanwhile, the Americans scheduled a host of meetings throughout the summer, apparently unaware that virtually all of Sweden takes off the month of July for vacation, or that Italians take off August. And in keeping with how everything else was going, even the computer systems proved incompatible.

While this may sound like a "Who's on first, What's on second" routine, people at Pharmacia & Upjohn weren't laughing. Merger and restructuring costs ran some $200 million higher than expected. Disagreements arose over where research should be carried out. Miscommunication between departments caused the delay of a product launch. And a large number of gifted R&D people at Pharmacia, fed up with the whole mess, left the company.[3]

Compare the 1998 Upjohn-Pharmacia merger with that of Price Waterhouse and Coopers & Lybrand into the world's largest accounting firm of Price Waterhouse Coopers. Prior to the merger, each firm had effectively served different segments of the market. Employees on each side obviously believed in the strategies they employed. Efforts to impose either firm's style on the other could have resulted in foot-dragging resistance aggravated by anxiety over whether the merger meant the elimination of jobs. Instead, an enlightened—and very Alexandrian—management strategy blended the best of each firm's culture into a new entity in which neither firm dominated. Even in the filling of top management positions in the new company, top jobs were allocated equally between managers from the

merging firms. In addition, much like Alexander's assurance to
local leaders that they would not be deposed, management
made sure all employees understood that their vision of growth
for the company meant more—not fewer—jobs. The strategy
worked. Few individuals left the newly created firm, evidence
that Alexander's emphasis on generating goodwill among
acquired partners was indeed sound assimilation policy.[4]

ALEXANDER'S MERGER SECRETS

Plutarch's biography of Alexander the Great reminds business
leaders that care must be taken in managing a merger or
acquisition. Alexander's emphasis on collaboration, on ruling
with—not over—the leaders of acquired territories (read companies), and on blending the best of each organization's culture
and talent is as critical to the successful melding of different
organizations as it was to the assimilation of different countries
and cultures. If this melding does not occur, the resulting
tensions often prevent hoped-for synergies (economies of
scale, technology transfer, more efficient sourcing, etc.) from
materializing.

The crucial point is to recognize that the first effect of a
merger is profound people trauma, and that the wounds can be
slow to heal. Employees are traumatized because their psychological contract has been broken. It is not surprising that they
feel betrayed. An "us-versus-them" attitude breeds defensive
behavior that is often damaging to both organizations. This
defensive behavior must be neutralized by an explicit strategy
that ensures continuity, demonstrates respect for the values and

mores of the acquired organization, and crisply identifies the new organization's goals. Only then can all employees understand exactly where they fit in under the "new arrangement."

One approach is to establish task forces made up of employees of the acquiring and acquired companies to address how best to integrate operations. That was the strategy employed by Praxair's president, Ed Hotard, when the company acquired CBI Industries. In an effort to build trust among CBI employees as they became part of Praxair, and to create bonds between employees of both companies, Hotard initiated the very Alexandrian strategy of "intermixture and association." Teams comprising Praxair and CBI employees were created at all levels of the organization to determine how best to integrate CBI's carbon dioxide business into Praxair. Said Hotard, himself a member of one of the teams, "We knew we had to reach clear objectives in a very short time, and we had to work together to do it. It helped the group bond together." This bonding among groups from the top of the organization on down created the beginnings of a new organizational culture that embraced employees of both firms.[5]

Perhaps most important, the old "don't fix it if it ain't broken" adage certainly applies—advice followed by Joe Guglielmi as chief executive of Taligent, the software joint venture between IBM and Apple. Although the new company was not the result of a corporate merger, Guglielmi faced the same task confronting many leaders of mergers or acquisitions: uniting employees from two very different organizational cultures into a new corporate culture. Most of Taligent's employees came from Apple and other Silicon Valley firms where a relaxed culture and individual empowerment were the norm. Guglielmi, a thirty-year IBM veteran, understood that imposing Big Blue's hierarchical structure and more formal culture on Taligent would cause a major exodus of employees.

His solution? Certainly one Alexander would have endorsed. Guglielmi determined those aspects of IBM's culture critical to the success of the new venture, worked to integrate these with Apple's operating strategy, and left the rest of Apple's culture intact. When asked whether he would institute a dress code at Taligent, for example, Guglielmi's response made it clear he wasn't interested in changing something that worked: "I told them I wouldn't comment on the way they dressed if they wouldn't comment on the way I dressed."[6]

Fabius
When Delay Is the Best Decision

Conventional wisdom has it that one of the things separating good managers from also-rans is their ability to make decisions quickly and take fast action. These dynamos, so goes the popular belief, reliably ferret out the best from an astonishing number of plausible possibilities. Like all other myths, this one is a blend of fact and invention. Nonetheless, leadership mythology celebrates the fast track in everything, imploring leaders to think fast, decide fast, act fast. "Don't sit around and worry about it; do something!" It's the stuff of overachievers and workaholics.

So much for the stereotype. The dull truth, it turns out, is that the best decisions are often the mind-numbingly slow ones.

The process of decision making—*good* decision making and the implementing actions that follow—can be a sluggish game indeed, much like, say, a British cricket game that goes on for days, the players taking civilized pauses for tea.

THINKING TAKES TIME

Maybe this was what was on Mark Twain's mind when he wryly observed that we should never put off till tomorrow what we could do the day after tomorrow just as well. True, that sentiment may never replace business's compelling time-is-money imperative, but there *are* occasions when a well-thought-out decision to delay taking action can make the difference between success and failure.

Chester Barnard, onetime president of the Rockefeller Foundation and New Jersey Bell, said it well. Often the best decision may be "not to decide. This is a most frequent decision, and from some points of view probably the most important. The fine art of executive decision consists in not deciding questions that are not now pertinent, in not deciding prematurely, in not making decisions that cannot be made effective, and in not making decisions that others should make."[7] Put more simply, when it comes to making decisions, speed is *not* everything.

Take that revered IBM motto "THINK," for example. It wasn't conceived to accelerate decision making. Quite the opposite. Plastered throughout the company's offices (even in the washrooms!) at founder T. J. Watson's insistence, "THINK" signs once implored IBM managers to slow down: to think first and then—*only* then—to act. Although Watson believed that thinking was useless unless it resulted in action, any IBMer guilty of shooting from the hip was committing an unpardonable sin.

Another believer in slowing the pace of decision making is management consultant Jack Falvey. After observing how managers "calendarize" every minute of every day, Falvey challenged the go-fast myth. "Your job is not to fill every waking moment with effort," says Falvey. "Your job is to achieve results, and if you are a manager, that means through the efforts of others. You can't be sensitive to others if you are constantly busy." Falvey urges leaders to cross several items off their leather-bound "to do" lists. "It's almost magic how much time you can create with that method."[8]

THINK-ing over the Organization's Survival

The story of Fabius, a Roman consul in the third century B.C., is a classic example of management by delayed action. He had the unlucky job of being one of Rome's rulers when Hannibal was crossing the Alps and fast approaching Italy's heartland. According to Plutarch, only a few of his fellow Romans believed that he would be up to the task:

> His slowness in speaking, his long labor and pains in learning, his deliberation in entering into the sports of other children, his easy submission to everybody, as if he had no will of his own, made those who judge superficially of him, the greater number, esteem him insensible and stupid; and few only saw that this tardiness

proceeded from stability, and discerned the greatness of his mind, and the lion-likeness of his temper.

Fabius may have been slow. But he was no dullard, as his critics soon discovered:

> As soon as he came into employment, his virtues exerted and showed themselves; his reputed want of energy then was recognized by people in general as a freedom of passion; his slowness in words and actions, the effect of a true prudence; his want of rapidity and his sluggishness, as constancy and firmness.

Fabius was caught in a bind. The Romans, panicked by fear of Hannibal's imminent attack, demanded just what Fabius was unwilling to give them: a quick decision and fast action. The city's politicians urged an immediate response. One general (with the remarkably appropriate name of "Flaminius") rushed north. Flaminius hoped to block the southerly advance of the Carthaginians, but they evaded him and broke through an unguarded pass in the Apennine hills. At Lake Trasimeno, disaster struck when Flaminius found himself surrounded on three sides by Hannibal's men. His impulsiveness had caused a rout. Thirty thousand of his men were killed or taken prisoner by Hannibal's army, and Flaminius himself was captured.

Fabius's strategy was different. He knew that the Carthaginians' supply lines were stretched to their limit, and he resolved to cut them off by devastating the surrounding countryside. He would avoid risking his armies in any pitched battles,

shadowing Hannibal closely instead as he headed south. Fabius
believed that delay, not fast action, would save Rome:

> Fabius . . . thought it not seasonable to engage with the
> enemy; . . . in regard that the Carthaginians were but
> few, and in want of money and supplies, he deemed it
> best not to meet in the field a general whose army had
> been tried in many encounters, and whose object was a
> battle, but to send aid to their allies, control the move-
> ments of the various subject cities, and let the force and
> vigor of Hannibal waste away and expire, like a flame,
> . for want of [nourishment].
>
> He set forth to oppose Hannibal, not with intention
> to fight him, but with the purpose of wearing out and
> wasting the vigor of his arms by lapse of time, of meet-
> ing his want of resources by superior means, by large
> numbers the smallness of his forces. With this design, he
> always encamped on the highest grounds, where the
> enemy's cavalry could have no access to him. Still he
> kept pace with them: when they marched, he followed
> them; when they encamped, he did the same, but at
> such a distance as not to be compelled to an engage-
> ment, and always keeping upon the hills, free from the
> insults of their horse, by which means he gave them no
> rest, but kept them in a continual alarm.

When Fabius decided to wait instead of rushing to attack
Hannibal, his fellow Romans were outraged. They accused him
of cowardice and nicknamed him "Cunctator" ("the Delayer").

Even his staff tried to convince him that he should quickly attack Hannibal, if for no other reason than to improve his popularity with the army and the Roman citizenry. According to Plutarch, Fabius responded by saying:

> "I should be more fainthearted than they make me, if, through fear of idle reproaches, I should abandon my own convictions. It is no inglorious thing to have fear for the safety of our country, but to be turned from one's course by men's opinions, by blame, and by misrepresentation, shows a man unfit to hold an office such as this."

The Romans wanted a quick fix, but it was the delaying strategy of Fabius that saved Rome. Knowing that time was his ally and Hannibal's greatest enemy, he turned that knowledge to his own advantage. It worked. Hannibal finally withdrew from Italy, unable to supply his forces adequately.

THE VIRTUES OF WAITING

Fabius proved that delaying action is not always bad. Indeed, waiting because the time is unfavorable is a sure sign of boldness, not timidity. Fabius also demonstrated that there is wisdom in taking the time necessary to make a well-reasoned decision, even when everyone else is clamoring for action.

At least two present-day management pundits agree. Peter Drucker, whose prolific writing has become something of a bible for leaders-to-be, argues that rapid-fire decision making ought to be discouraged. In *The Effective Executive*, he summarily dismisses it as a symptom of "sloppy thinking."[9] And Allan Cox, who explores the differences between Japanese and American management in *The Making of the Achiever*, charges that the main problem with American managers is their tendency to superfast decision making. "What we American executives often do *not do* is digest," he says. "We handle. Quickly. We don't think. We don't ask apparently absurd questions to see if we can discover profound connections and relationships in the order of things. We don't because we don't have the time. We're too busy *doing*."[10]

The views of Drucker and Cox imply that when someone boasts that he or she is a fast decision maker, it's best to take cover and warn others to do the same. And as Cox noted, failure to take the time to examine a decision from every angle can lead to precipitous action—when delaying action might have been the wiser choice. Pfizer Inc.'s 1998 introduction of its impotency drug, Viagra, is a case in point. When Viagra proved effective in overcoming male impotence, there was no question the company had a winner. A vigorous advertising and public relations campaign accompanied by extensive media hype created a frenzied demand for the drug—nearly two million new prescriptions were written in the first two months after it became available. In those same two months, however, the deaths of sixteen men taking Viagra were also reported. While Pfizer and FDA officials continued to proclaim the drug safe, concern mounted about unforeseen side effects and adverse interactions with other drugs—especially ones commonly prescribed to treat prostate and cardiovascular problems. Pfizer had chosen not to include most of these drugs when testing Viagra for drug interactions, prompting questions about whether adequate testing on drug interactions had been carried out. Such is the need for speed caused by the pharmaceutical industry's ever-faster "time-to-market" cycle.[11]

It was Fabius's decision to go ploddingly that prevented Hannibal from capturing Rome. Adopting the Fabian strategy of slowing the decision process down may be counterintuitive when you're trying to get an exciting new product to market, but it can save bundles in negative publicity and liability exposure. Fabius is no longer remembered as a coward, or even as a "delayer." He proved that in management, as in politics and war, "delay" does not have to be a dirty word.

THREE

PLATO

The Philosopher-Manager

When Alfred North Whitehead said that the West's philosophical tradition consists merely of a series of footnotes to "him," he was referring to Plato, the Greek philosopher born in 428 B.C. Another devotee, Ralph Waldo Emerson, had rhapsodized a century before Whitehead: "Burn all the libraries, for their value is in this one book." Emerson was referring to Plato's most famous work, *The Republic.*

These laudatory opinions of Plato are almost universally shared. He, along with Socrates, his teacher, and Aristotle, his student, laid the philosophical foundations of Western culture. Plato developed a discerning and wide-ranging system of thought that was at once ethical, mystical, and rational. Against the profound intellectual confusion and moral chaos following

Athens's defeat in the Peloponnesian War, Plato's philosophical system offered the solace of absolute ethical principles: a strong anchor, as it were, against turbulent and frightening change. Indeed, if the Periclean Age had been all that its supporters claimed it was, or if the Peloponnesian War had not sapped Athenian will, Plato's greatest dialogues might never have been written.

But Plato did write—prodigiously. His dialogues, after 2,400 years, are still incomparable studies of the basic issues that confront human beings. They offer even more—particularly to those who manage and lead—because their author was not only a consummate philosopher but also an accomplished manager, innovator, and entrepreneur. The school he established in Athens in 387 B.C. as an institute for the systematic pursuit of philosophical and scientific research was an entrepreneurial triumph, lasting more than 500 years. It was a true educational innovation in that tedious lecturing was mercifully not allowed. Instead, students, egged on by their teachers, discussed, argued, and analyzed "problems," much as their twenty-first-century counterparts come to grips with cases at many business schools today.

The only biographical knowledge we have of Plato comes from some of his letters. We know that he had a refined palate and enjoyed the art of living life to its fullest, became an aristocratic Greek, and was a man of exquisite taste with a great love of beauty. Plato was blessed with a keen mind and a good sense of humor. In short, Plato possessed all of the accoutrements that one might expect in a successful young man. He wasted none of them. At twenty-five, he was a poet and playwright. At forty, he had founded his Academy. By the end of his life (he died in his eighties), he had written more than thirty-five works.

As a young man, Plato had his heart set on a career in politics. But he soon became disenchanted with this idea. Why he turned to philosophy is evident in one of his letters:

> I, who had at first been full of eagerness for a public career, as I gazed upon the whirlpool of public life and saw the incessant movement of shifting currents, at last felt dizzy . . . and finally saw clearly in regard to all states now existing that without exception their system of government is bad.

This critical appraisal of the human condition animated much of Plato's philosophy. Especially in his later life, Plato was motivated largely by frustration and even despair. The disastrous Peloponnesian War affected him deeply, as had the death of his mentor, Socrates. He was infuriated by the incompetence of Pericles' successors, and he was outraged by the rising influence of Sparta, whose culture was almost the opposite of that of Athens.

History's First Consultant's Report

Plato was a reformer. He sought to change Athens, just as any contemporary manager wants to "turn around" a troubled organization. This is what makes Plato's most famous dialogue, *The Republic*, superb reading for managers as well as philosophers.

It is history's first consultant's report to the leaders of an organization that is being badly beaten by the competition.

The Republic was a response to this catastrophic management failure. In it, Plato argued against the management style of Periclean Athens. He saw it as a kind of destructive imbalance, a style of managing in which self-serving individual interests could too easily overwhelm the needs of the organization. He challenged assumptions about management and leadership that were as voguish in ancient Athens as they are in our society, reaffirmed others, and established wholly new ones. *The Republic* focuses on Plato's critical appraisal of democratic management and provides an excellent example of Socratic dialectic.

"Democratic" Management
Plato's Second Opinion

Managing "democratically" has been at the heart of American management since the 1960s. Although individual interpretations vary somewhat, there is a common thread: managers are exhorted to become more people-oriented and employees are encouraged to participate in decision making. The goal is the de-emphasis of "top-down," autocratic decision making in favor of a "bottom-up," participative style.

Democratic management has been an appealing, and uniquely American, idea. In line with the West's egalitarian political philosophy, it has been programmed into corporate cultures by management consultants, professed by business school teachers, and touted in corporate training programs. Its most influential devotee, twentieth-century behavioral scientist Douglas McGregor, has been permanently enshrined in the pantheon of management scholars.

But Does Democratic Management Work?

Plato's reservations about the effectiveness of democratic leadership in fifth-century B.C. Athens may be useful to consider today. Whether or not one agrees with Plato's criticism of democratic management, his position provides a provocative "second opinion." Plato had been deeply offended by the immoderation of radical Athenian democracy. He had observed Athenian leaders being seduced into giving the people whatever they wanted. Athens was moving increasingly in the direction of becoming a welfare state. Plato saw thousands of jurors, councilors, major and minor officials, and others gaining their livelihood from the public coffers. The boom in government buildings provided not only jobs, but also a rich architectural legacy that far outlasted the state institutions that the buildings were designed to house. In sum, the state's services became an entitlement, having been transformed from an activity that most could not afford to one that they welcomed and later demanded.

Plato's often-critical perspective on democratic management can be better understood against this troublesome background. He believed that although radical democracy may have been effective during Athens's golden age, it was an unalloyed disaster once storm clouds appeared on the horizon. He saw that a new kind of leader—a "philosopher-king"—might be the only solution.

Plato's critique of democratic management was wide-ranging. He feared the leadership of amateurs over professionals, the rise of excessive individualism, and the diffusion of responsibility that is the inevitable result of management by committee. More than anything else, he was haunted by the fear that radical democracy would inevitably lead to the appointment of leaders who cared more about flattering the mob than about doing what was right. Citizens, Plato noted, were often not the best judges of who should lead. Nowhere are these doubts better described than in his parable of the ship's navigator:

> The sailors are quarreling over the control of the helm.
> . . . They do not understand that the genuine navigator
> can only make himself fit to command a ship by study-
> ing the seasons of the year, sky, stars, and winds, and all
> that belongs to his craft; and they have no idea that,
> along with the science of navigation, it is possible for
> him to gain, by instruction or practice, the skill to keep
> control of the helm whether some of them like it or not.
> If a ship were managed in that way, would not those on
> board be likely to call the expert in navigation a mere
> stargazer, who spent his time in idle talk and was useless
> to them?

Plato's ship is like any organization wracked by factionalism. People mill around waiting for someone to take charge, often choosing the most popular, but not the best qualified, among them as leader. Like the true navigator in the parable, the most competent candidate for manager will rarely be selected by the employees.

ONE ORGANIZATION VERSUS MANY

Plato believed that radical democracy would inevitably lead to chaos, resulting in an organization made up of "many organizations," in which each would go its own independent way:

> Now what is the character of this new regime? Obviously the way they govern themselves will throw light on the democratic type of man.
>
> No doubt.
>
> First of all, they are free. Liberty and free speech are rife everywhere; anyone is allowed to do what he likes.
>
> Yes, so we are told.
>
> That being so, every man will arrange his own manner of life to suit his pleasure. The result will be a greater variety of individuals than under any other constitution. So it may be the finest of all, with its variegated pattern of all sorts of characters. Many people may think it the best, just as women and children might admire a mixture of colors of every shade in the pattern of a dress. . . . There is so much tolerance and superiority to petty considerations; such a contempt for all those fine principles we laid down in founding our commonwealth, as when we said that only a very exceptional

nature could turn out a good man, if he had not played as a child among things of beauty and given himself only to creditable pursuits. A democracy tramples all such notions under foot; with a magnificent indifference to the sort of life a man has led before he enters politics, it will promote to honor anyone who merely calls himself the people's friend.

Plato believed that in management—of states or other organizations—someone has to take responsibility. Someone has to call the shots and lead. This does not mean that managers or other leaders have to be callous, thoughtless, or inhumane. It does, however, require singleness of purpose, loyalty to a vision of what the organization is to become, and a great deal of self-discipline.

THE NEED FOR BENEVOLENT TYRANTS

Plato was perceptive enough to see that leading must sometimes be a solo act, that leaders must be more concerned with the good of the enterprise than with pleasing the multitude. On those frequent occasions when the two are compatible, an easygoing, democratic, management-by-consensus style works and works well. But Plato knew that when the going gets tough, it might be time for a benevolent tyrant to take the helm.

A tough-minded leader might have saved the old Studebaker Company, the now-defunct automobile maker. There are striking parallels between the downfall of Studebaker and the ancient clash of democratic Athens and autocratic Sparta.

Studebaker's demise was caused by its interest in furthering industrial democracy rather than in meeting the developing threat from General Motors. Managing by committee and making excessive concessions to its unions, Studebaker lost sight of its economic objectives. Meanwhile, GM focused with Spartan tenacity on the business of survival. Its authoritarianism worked. Today GM is the largest automaker in the world. Studebaker went out of business in 1964.

Compare the Studebaker case with a more recent example. Jack Harnett, president of D. L. Rogers Corp., which owns fifty-four Sonic Corp. drive-in restaurant franchises, could not be considered a democratic leader by any stretch of the imagination. There's one way to do things—his way—and he doesn't hesitate to tell employees that. "Do it the way we tell you to do it," Harnett tells his workers, while "I will only tell you one time," is the last of his eight guidelines to which employees must adhere. The guidelines are rigidly enforced; anyone who breaks the same commandment twice is shown the door. Likewise, employees who use their own initiative without Harnett's approval earn his disapproval. As he explains it, "We have a success formula that works."

That formula includes motivating people by giving them what he says everyone wants: money. He pays his employees well, far above the industry norm; he also demands that they buy equity in the company's franchises but in return gives them a share of the net profits. His formula for managing people also includes becoming involved in their personal lives—whatever problems they're having he wants to know about and help solve. "I don't think [employees] can be totally focused on making money" if they go to work worried about what's happening at home or at school with their kids, he explains. He wants to know exactly what's going on in his eateries as well, often stopping by a restaurant unannounced to chat with customers, tour the facility, and "suggest" improvements that certainly will be made before he stops by again.

While Harnett's decidedly undemocratic style of leadership may leave some management experts uneasy, his success offers little reason for changing it. D. L. Rogers realizes more than $40 million in annual revenues from its franchises. Managers' and supervisors' average earnings—from salaries, a percentage of net profits, and bonuses for meeting goals determined by Harnett—are twice the industry average. Revenues per restaurant are far above the industry's norm, while turnover among managers and supervisors are far below it.[1]

As Plato suggested, democratic management is not a cure-all. It is not the only style of management that works. Giving everyone a vote is not always necessary: like the ship's crew in Plato's parable, employees may not know enough about what it is they are voting on to make the wisest choice. Good management is sometimes a solo act, relying less on democratic consensus than on individual judgment.

Nurturing Disagreement
Managing "Socratically"

Socrates, who lived from 470 B.C. to 399 B.C., was Plato's intellectual inspiration, teacher, and friend and the leading character in his dialogues. History views Socrates enthusiastically, and not unjustifiably, as the paragon of philosophy and its true father. But, as is often the case, his contemporaries were less impressed and quite unconscious of his greatness. To them he was, quite simply, the town character. Many wrote him off as an obtrusive bore due to his penchant for assaulting them with embarrassing questions. As if this were not enough, Socrates claimed to be under the guidance of a special "voice," declaring that he had received messages from the Delphic Oracle— an assertion that greatly increased both his local importance and his notoriety. He was a popular pedagogue who gathered around him a clique of young disciples. Together they frequented Athens's marketplace and out-talked all but their sturdiest companions.

As self-appointed gadfly, Socrates spent most of his life causing no end of trouble in complacent, conservative Athens. By questioning, cajoling, wheedling, and prodding, he forced Athenians to think and to question beliefs that they had taken for granted. This finally got him into trouble. The Athenians charged him with impiety toward the gods and corrupting the youth. He was thrown into prison, tried, and sentenced to death. After a month, during which he refused friends' offers to help him escape, Socrates drank a cup of hemlock and died.

THE IMPORTANCE OF QUESTIONING

Socrates left humankind an immensely valuable legacy: the "Socratic method" of question and answer. He was firmly convinced that the human mind could arrive at virtue and truth only through a process of questioning and discussion. He was, above all else, an incomparable questioner and an exceptional listener—perhaps the best arguer the world has ever known. He knew that asking the right questions was far more important than getting the right answers. Questioning was Socrates' way of getting at the truth at the core of a problem. Using dialectic, he would examine opinions or ideas logically and from many points of view, much as a jeweler looks at a gem from many angles in order to determine its value.

In *The Republic*, Plato's characters are invariably trying to discover the truth through the use of dialectic. One states an opinion. Another criticizes it. This dialogue takes a lot of time. The impatient reader gets the idea that Plato's characters, unlike busy managers, have all the time in the world. They go off on what seem to be irrelevant tangents. There is no agenda. No schedule. And there are many "meetings." In other words, dialectic not only requires Job-like patience but also seems to be the opposite of "good management."

AN EXAMPLE OF MANAGING BY ASKING QUESTIONS

In *The Republic*, Socrates' dialogue with Polemarchus on the meaning of justice demonstrates dialectic in action. A member of the group, Simonides, has already argued that justice means "giving every man his due." Socrates argues that Simonides surely did not mean it "just," for example, to return dangerous weapons to a madman simply because they were owed to him.

Notice in the following excerpts how, through the process of cross-examination, Socrates gets Polemarchus to make certain admissions, then step-by-step draws him on, and finally leads him to reach an absurd conclusion—which exposes the fallacy of his argument:

> "It is certainly hard to question the inspired wisdom of a poet like Simonides; but what this saying means you may know, Polemarchus, but I do not. Obviously it does not mean what we were speaking of just now—returning something we have been entrusted with to the owner even when he has gone out of his mind. And yet surely it is his due, if he asks for it back?"
>
> "Yes."
>
> "But it is out of the question to give it back when he has gone mad?"
>
> "True."
>
> "Simonides, then, must have meant something different from that when he said it was just to render a man his due."
>
> "Certainly he did."

Socrates then shows that Simonides' definition of justice, to "return that which is owed," cannot apply in this case, since only "good" is due from one friend to another:

> "And what about enemies? Are we to render whatever is their due to them?"

"Yes, certainly, what really is due to them; which
means, I suppose, what is appropriate to an enemy—
some sort of injury."

"It seems, then, that Simonides was using words
with a hidden meaning, as poets will. He really meant
to define justice as rendering to everyone what is appropriate to him; only he called that his 'due.'"

"Well, why not?"

Now Polemarchus changes the course of the discussion to
the meaning of justice among enemies:

"His idea was that, as between friends, what one owes
to another is to do him good, not harm."

"I see," said I; "to repay money entrusted to one is
not to render what is due, if the two parties are friends
and the repayment proves harmful to the lender. That is
what you say Simonides meant?"

"Yes, certainly."

At this point, Socrates satirizes the common Greek belief
that justice consists of helping one's friends and harming one's
enemies, by constructing an analogy between justice and the
arts. He leads Polemarchus to conclude that the "work" of justice is the giving of good to friends and evil to enemies, just as
the "work" of medicine gives health to human bodies:

"But look here," said I. "Suppose we could question
Simonides about the art of medicine—whether a physician can be described as rendering to some object what

is due or appropriate to it; how do you think he would answer?"

"That the physician administers the appropriate diet or remedies to the body."

"And the art of cookery—can that be described in the same way?"

"Yes; the cook gives the appropriate seasoning to his dishes."

"Good. And the practice of justice?"

"If we are to follow those analogies, Socrates, justice would be rendering services or injuries to friends or enemies."

"So Simonides means by justice doing good to friends and harm to enemies?"

"I think so."

"And in matters of health, who would be the most competent to treat friends and enemies in that way?"

"A physician."

"And on a voyage, as regards the dangers of the sea?"

"A ship's captain."

"In what sphere of action, then, will the just man be the most competent to do good or harm?"

"In war, I should imagine; when he is fighting on the side of his friends and against his enemies."

"I see. But when we are well and staying on shore, the doctor and the ship's captain are of no use to us."

"True."

"It is also true that the just man is useless when we are not at war?"

"I should not say that."

Polemarchus is subsequently reduced to asserting that the "work" of justice is the safekeeping of money when it is not being used. That is, justice does not serve a very important function:

"So, justice has its uses in peacetime, too?"

"Yes."

"Like farming, which is useful for producing crops, or shoe making, which is useful for providing us with shoes. Can you tell me for what purposes justice is useful or profitable in time of peace?"

"For matters of business, Socrates."

"In a partnership, you mean?"

"Yes."

"But if we are playing draughts, or laying bricks, or making music, will the just man be as good and helpful a partner as an expert draught player, or a builder, or a musician?"

"No."

"Then, in what kind of partnership will he be more helpful?"

"Where money is involved, I suppose."

"Except, perhaps, Polemarchus, when we are putting our money to some use. If we are buying or selling a horse, a judge of horses would be a better partner; or if we are dealing in ships, a shipwright or a sea captain."

"I suppose so."

"Well, when will the just man be specially useful in handling our money?"

"When we want to deposit it for safekeeping."

"When the money is to lie idle, in fact?"

"Yes."

"So, justice begins to be useful only when our money is out of use?"

"Perhaps so."

Socrates, using dialectic, has led Polemarchus to recognize the vagueness of his—and Simonides'—ideas about justice by demonstrating to him the absurdity of his initial conclusions.

Socratic Management at General Electric

Likewise, managers can adapt Socratic dialectic to improve critical thinking and the quality of communications in their organizations. It's a method Jack Welch, legendary chairman and chief executive of General Electric Co., has adapted and honed to perfection. Meetings with Jack, as everyone at GE calls him, are what one executive described as "free-for-alls"—spirited dialogues in which Welch questions, probes, debates, and challenges, and expects everyone else to do the same. Whether meeting with the corporation's executive officers, top executives, managers, or would-be managers, Welch uses dialectic to test people, strategies, assumptions, and expectations, and he relishes the lively and candid debates that get communication—and ideas—flowing. Ideas, after all, are ultimately what Welch is after.

"The idea flow from the human spirit is absolutely unlimited," says Welch. "All you have to do is tap into that well." It's obvious Welch and thousands of GE employees have tapped into that well time and again: under Welch's leadership, the market value of the gigantic corporation, with businesses in more than 100 countries, has increased more than 2,300 percent. What Welch has done, of course, is not just tap into that unlimited flow of ideas, but—much like Socrates—used dialectic to examine, refine, and test those ideas in order to arrive at "the truth."[2]

Peter Drucker, in *The Effective Executive*, also endorses the use of Socratic dialectic in management. "Decisions of the kind the executive has to make," he says, "are not made well by acclamation. They are made well only if based on the clash of conflicting views, the dialogue between different points of view, the choice between different judgments. The first rule in decision making is that one does not make a decision unless there is disagreement."[3] Alfred P. Sloan, the man who revitalized General Motors in the 1920s when it was close to bankruptcy, appreciated the value of dialogue versus monologue. At a meeting of one of his top committees, everyone assented to the proposal being considered. "Gentlemen," retorted Sloan, "I take it we are all in complete agreement on the decision here." Everyone around the conference table nodded. "Then," he continued, "I propose we postpone further discussion on this matter until our next meeting to give ourselves time to develop disagreement and perhaps gain some understanding of what the decision is all about."

NURTURE DISAGREEMENT; NURTURE DIALOGUE

The lesson of all this is to avoid the managerial monologue and to engage instead in dialogue. Leadership, it turns out, is surprisingly similar to philosophy. It requires engaged inquiry. Like the participants in Plato's dialogues, leaders must get people to feel the challenge of a problem that involves them. Only dialogue makes this possible. Policy manuals and detailed procedures cannot replace the spirited inquiry that is consistently produced via dialogue. It's important, too, to learn to listen and to question. This may sound simple, but it is very hard to do. Most managers lecture. They tell. This has its place, of course, for they must pass on their experience to others. As an information-disseminating device, the monologue works reasonably well. But as a problem-solving device, it is a disaster.

Socratic dialogue is a learnable communications strategy of immense importance to leaders. It is *the* critical element in a strong, centralized management system like the one Plato advocated. It enables the whole organization system, from "philosopher-manager" to newest employee, to get to the truth. The organization's history, experience, and "truths" are passed down from executives to junior managers through dialogue. And the junior manager's perceptions of his or her problems are similarly passed up the organization. Dialogue demands one-on-one communications. It demands feedback. It demands that cherished assumptions be continually challenged. And it "licenses" tough-minded management that is based on fact, not opinion.

FOUR

PERICLES

Father of Corporate Culture

A mong an astonishingly large assortment of leadership fads and fashions that pass into and out of vogue in business management, "corporate culture" is one of the most popular. Everyone is rushing to get on the bandwagon. One board chairman's comment, reported in *Business Week*, is typical: "This corporate culture stuff is great," he exclaimed after listening to a consultant's presentation. "I want a culture by next Monday."[1]

That executive might be surprised to learn that corporate culture has been around for more than 2,000 years. A man who believed that he had discovered the ideal balance between individual and organization—Pericles, the father of Athens's golden age—first articulated it. Although celebrated by historians as a man of unchallengeable virtue and greatness, Pericles was also an enigmatic and contradictory figure. His policies helped bring

Athens to its zenith, yet it was his imperialistic expansion that ultimately caused its destruction. He is remembered as the man who perfected Athenian democracy, but early in his career he supported an exclusivist law limiting citizenship to those of Athenian parentage. He built the architecture that made Athens one of the world's most beautiful cities and has dominated our idea of public building ever since, but he did so with a desire to stimulate Athens's economy and to celebrate in marble the glory of Athens. Unfortunately, funding came not from internally generated cash flow, but from the treasuries of Athens's allies. Their growing resentment and neighboring Sparta's fear of Athens's growing power culminated in the Peloponnesian War, which ultimately destroyed Athens. Nonetheless, Pericles is rightly credited with securing Athens's political and cultural leadership in Greece, even if for a brief period. Part of Pericles' success must be attributed to his deep understanding of, and his ability to articulate, what we now refer to as "corporate culture."

The best statement of Pericles' position is evidenced in a speech he made in 431 or 430 B.C. at a funeral ceremony for soldiers who had died in the first year of the Peloponnesian War. Pericles knew that Athens's survival might depend on his ability to unify the Athenians. He seized this opportunity to sketch an idealized picture of his society, much as Lincoln did at Gettysburg 2,300 years later. Pericles' speech is one of history's finest statements of an organization's shared values and beliefs— its culture. It demonstrates that establishing a strong corporate culture (in both modern and ancient societies) requires two things. First, a leader must determine what it is that makes the organization different. Second, he or she must effectively and eloquently communicate that difference to the organization's members.

Identifying What Makes the Organization Different

Pericles focused on four cultural characteristics that made Athens unique.

1. He first exalted the positive aspects of Athenian life—its openness, its democratic style, and its optimistic estimate of people's capabilities and potentials. He made it clear that membership in the Athenian organization was supremely valuable: Athenian citizenship was the greatest prize a person could gain; the constitution of Athens was not a mere collection of legalisms, but a mode of life. He underscored the importance of democracy, of job selection and promotion based solely on merit, and of the primacy of individual dignity:

> [We are] called a democracy because power is in the hands not of a minority but of the whole people. When it is a question of settling private disputes, everyone is equal before the law; when it is a question of putting one person before another in positions of public responsibility, what counts is not membership of a particular class, but the actual ability that the man possesses. . . . And, just as our political life is free and open, so is our day-to-day life in our relations with each other. We do not get into a state with our next-door neighbor if he

enjoys himself in his own way, nor do we give him the
kind of black looks which, though they do no real harm,
still do hurt people's feelings. We are free and tolerant in
our private lives, but in public affairs we keep to the law.
This is because it commands our deep respect.

2. In words strikingly suggestive of the "work hard, play
hard" corporate cultures in vogue today, Pericles next emphasized the importance of just having a good time:

> When our work is over, we are in a position to enjoy all
> kinds of recreation for our spirits. There are various
> kinds of contests and sacrifices regularly throughout the
> year; in our own homes we find a beauty and good taste
> which delight us every day and which drive away our
> cares.

3. Pericles gave his listeners further cause for pride in their
organization by reminding them that Athens was an opinion
leader, an innovator. Athens did not emulate its competitors.
Indeed, it set the standard that others followed. Athens, he said,

> does not copy the institutions of our neighbors. It is
> more a case of our being a model to others than of our
> imitating anyone else.
>
> There is a great difference between us and our oppo-
> nents, in our attitude toward military security. Here are
> some examples: Our city is open to the world, and we
> have no periodical deportations in order to prevent peo-
> ple observing or finding out secrets that might be of mil-

itary advantage to the enemy. This is because we rely, not on secret weapons, but on our own real courage and loyalty. There is a difference, too, in our educational system. The Spartans, from their earliest boyhood, are submitted to the most laborious training in courage; we pass our lives without all these restrictions and yet are just as ready to face the same dangers as they are. . . . There are certain advantages, I think, in our way of meeting danger voluntarily, with an easy mind, instead of with a laborious training, with natural rather than with state-induced courage.

4. Finally, in an eloquent summation of Athens's corporate culture, Pericles emphasized the balance achieved between the individual and the organization:

Here each individual is interested not only in his own affairs but in the affairs of the state as well: even those who are mostly occupied with their own business are extremely well informed on general politics. This is a peculiarity of ours: we do not say that a man who takes no interest in politics is a man who minds his own business; we say that he has no business here at all. . . .

. . . Taking everything together then, I declare that our city is an education to Greece. . . . You should fix your eyes every day on the greatness of Athens as she really is, and should fall in love with her.

If this sounds passé, think again. Ancient organizations aren't the only ones that have found creeds invaluable. When the former Marriott International, Inc., spun off a new public company named Marriott International, comprising its lodging, senior living, and food distribution businesses, the fledgling enterprise needed to delineate its own identity. Yet, it was important to tie the new corporation to Marriott's original founding principles. Two simple sentences in the 1997 annual report to shareholders did just that, providing a clear description of the new company's culture:

> We combine the energy and enthusiasm of a new enterprise with the Marriott traditions of service and value which have guided us for more than seven decades.
> We are steadfastly dedicated to providing exceptional service to our customers, growth opportunities for our associates, and attractive returns to our stockholders and owners.[2]

Equally clear shared values exist at such companies as Hewlett-Packard (key value: innovation), IBM (key values: respect for the individual, customer service, superior performance), Procter & Gamble (key value: product quality), and 3M (key value: innovation).

One modern description of corporate culture, however, has many similarities to Pericles' description of the culture of Athens:

> In an environment—and an industry—that is changing at an accelerating pace, companies must be flexible, independent, and capable of making the right decisions. In turn, this requires flexible and independent employ-

ees who can—and dare to—make their own decisions. Do IT (Decisive, Open, Innovative, and Trusting) is the name of . . . [our] corporate culture, based on several common values.

Decisive: Use resources effectively. The person with the right knowledge makes the decisions—this is a privilege, a right, and an obligation. Dare to take initiatives and to act independently.

Open: Be open to challenges. Work together with others, seek out and distribute information and experiences across organizational boundaries—for the benefit of customers and the company. Express your own opinions.

Innovative: Take initiatives; champion ideas that you believe in. Work with the customer's expectations and needs. Ideas and suggestions are encouraged, respected, and rewarded.

Trusting: Have confidence in yourself, your colleagues and . . . [the company]. Follow through on your commitments, both internally and with customers—you must earn customers' trust. Mistakes are allowed, but accept responsibility for correction and learning from them.

This statement was written more than 2,400 years after Pericles' speech. Yet it serves the same purpose at Ericsson Data, a worldwide supplier of telecommunications and related terminals, as Pericles' speech did in ancient Athens. It identifies the organization's unique characteristics. It defines the organization's culture.[3]

Communicating What Makes the
Organization Different

Identifying what made Athens different was not enough. Pericles also had to communicate that difference effectively. He was entirely up to the task, since he was one of the city's most capable orators. One of his biographers reported that Pericles'

> use of hopes and fears, as his two chief rudders, with one to check the [people's] confidence at any time, . . . the other to raise them up and cheer them when under any discouragement, plainly showed . . . that rhetoric, or the art of speaking, is . . . the government of the souls of men, and that [its] chief business is to address the affections and passions which are, as it were, the strings and keys to the soul, and require a skillful and careful touch to be played on as they should be.

Pericles' ability to identify and communicate Athens's uniqueness helped transform the Athenians into a cohesive group. He wanted Athenians to see that the good of the organization was more important than the good of the individual. The individual's success depended on the willingness of group members to cooperate with one another. That willingness became Athens's greatest strength and, rightly so, its primary source of pride.

Whether they are ancient Athenians threatened by Spartan competition, modern automakers tormented by the Japanese, or computer designers trying to capture the next innovation in technology, people need to know—and frequently be reminded of—what their organizations stand for, what makes them special, what makes them worth fighting for. This is done at General Electric, a company we've mentioned before, where Jack Welch often uses the analogy of a grocery store to invoke the informality of a small business in which people don't get bogged down in bureaucracy and in which knowing and serving customers' needs is what makes the business thrive. "What's important at the grocery store is just as important in engines or medical systems," he reminds employees. "If the customer isn't satisfied, if the stuff is getting stale, if the shelf isn't right, or if the offerings aren't right, it's the same thing. You manage like a small organization. You don't get hung up on zeros." Like Pericles, Welch knows that in order to forge his far-flung organization—containing companies as disparate as NBC and GE Plastics—into a unified organization, he must establish a common culture.[4]

Napoleon once said, "Human beings are controlled through their imaginations; that is what distinguishes them from animals. A soldier does not face death in order to earn a few pence a day, or to win some paltry order of merit. None but the man who touches his heart can stir his enthusiasm." Pericles knew how to touch the hearts of his fellow Athenians. He demonstrated that a leader must articulate the organization's ideology. Leaders like Pericles and executives at Marriott International, Ericsson Data, and General Electric have defined a coherent corporate culture in order to promote a sense of unity and purpose in their organizations. That definition reminds the organization's members (whether citizens or employees) of the kind of people they are, and—more important—the kind of people they are to become.

FIVE

SOPHOCLES

The Psychology of Leadership

The balance between the individual and the organization achieved by the Athenians was epitomized by Sophocles, an aristocratic, highly educated man whose name means "wise and honored one." Sophocles' play *Ajax* depicts what can happen when an individual's pride overwhelms his sense of responsibility to the organization. In *Antigone*, Sophocles describes the dual dangers of excessive persistence and inflexibility.

Not only did Sophocles (496–406 B.C.) achieve immortality as a playwright, but he also played, throughout his life, a full role in the affairs of Athens: he was the city's treasurer (charged with receiving and managing tribute money flowing in from Athens's more than 300 subject states), one of its top generals (an appointment some think he received because of the political wisdom revealed in his play *Antigone*), and a close colleague of Pericles, the father of Athens's golden age.

Sophocles, like Plato, was blessed with virtues universally admired in Athens. He possessed rare physical beauty—statues portray him as handsome and vigorous even in old age—and he was full of grace and charm. His athletic skill and musical talent enabled him to win an unusual double prize in wrestling and music competition. At sixteen, he was given the honor of leading Athenian youths in a celebration of the Greek victory over the Persians at the battle of Salamis. At twenty-eight, he won Athens's annual playwriting competition by defeating Aeschylus (until then Athens's leading playwright).

Sophocles was a master at interpreting individual human behavior and its effect on the organization. He depicted, with uncanny perception, great characters and the motives that shaped their behavior. He was such an accomplished student of the human psyche that two of his major characters, Electra and Oedipus, define the psychological disorders that bear their names.

Many of Sophocles' plays—in his long life he wrote 123 of them—reaffirm what astute managers already know: that an organization can flourish only if its individual and organizational needs converge. Likewise, these plays dramatize the grim consequences if this does not happen. Many scenes in Sophocles' plays demonstrate flaws that are the raw material of management failure: deceptive reports, rumors, false optimism, hasty judgment, and mistakes in planning, decision making, and communication. Sophocles' tragedies unforgettably illustrate the damage that can be done by usurping authority, abusing power, and lacking respect for others. But most important, they provide compelling evidence that individuals and organizations rise and fall unpredictably and that it is impossible to base effective management and leadership solely on that centerpiece of "scientific" management, rational calculation.

Ajax
Pride Goeth Before the Fall

The idea that the gods would slap down any mortal who became too powerful, rich, or ambitious was widespread among the ancient Greeks. "It is always the biggest buildings and the tallest trees that are struck by lightning," said the ancient Greek historian Herodotus. "The gods are accustomed to throw down whatever rises too high." Perhaps no play better dramatizes how devastatingly a deity can punish a person's tendency to arrogance and overweening pride than does Sophocles' play *Ajax*.

It is a story that is must reading for every manager who is "on a roll" that he or she believes will continue forever. And it is a story for anyone who is fascinated, as the Greeks certainly were, by the prospect of good fortune's being changed in the twinkling of an eye to abject adversity—of the great being brought down by influences over which they had little control.

The story takes place after the events described in Homer's *Iliad*. The Greeks' best warrior, Achilles, had been killed by a god-directed arrow aimed (by the Trojan warrior Paris) at what is now known as the Achilles tendon, and the disposition of his armor was now at issue. This may seem a trivial question to twenty-first-century readers, but it was vitally important to the

Greeks, who believed that whoever inherited a dead warrior's armor would be endowed with his strength and power—characteristics that, in the heroic age, superseded all others.

Ajax, who was considered the greatest Greek warrior after Achilles, had good reason to believe that he would inherit Achilles' armor. He was said to be like a lion, at the beginning of a battle, and like a stubborn mule when he was forced back by superior numbers. Opposing soldiers were awed by him. Homer described an enemy king's apprehension upon seeing Ajax towering over the attacking forces outside the walls of his town:

> "Who is that great and goodly warrior whose head and broad shoulders tower above the rest of the Greeks?"
>
> "That," answered Helen, "is huge Ajax, bulwark of the Greeks."

KEEPING UP WITH A CHANGING ORGANIZATION

Sophocles portrays Ajax as the unfortunate person who is unable, or unwilling, to adapt to a changing organization. The Greek leaders at Troy decided not to award Achilles' armor to Ajax, because they were looking for a new kind of person to receive this honor: someone who was more than just the best warrior, someone who would represent the organization's new ideals and values. They wanted this honor to reflect a new balance in the relationship between individual and organization. Superb on-the-job performance was no longer the only thing that counted.

The Greek leaders recognized that Ajax was enormously valuable and that he had proved his worth on countless occasions. At any other time, he would have received their highest honor. But he represented an old code of behavior that, in Sophocles' view, was fast becoming outmoded. It was a code based on strict discipline, stability, and rigidity, and for hundreds of years it had served as an ideal of Greek life. It distrusted mere talk and esteemed action instead. It placed greater value on individualism than on the needs of the organization. But it contained a corrosive tinge of self-destruction, a tendency to excess, a need to outdo not only oneself but everyone else as well, and—perhaps most damning—an inclination toward settling disagreements not by reason but by battle.

The Greek leaders concluded—and they were correct— that Ajax was *not* their man. As the inheritor of Achilles' armor, they chose Odysseus, who in a later age would have been a model "organization man." Odysseus was adaptable where Ajax was unyielding. He was inventive. He believed in the power of reason over brute force. He was a man of stratagem and guile. And he was an eloquent speaker who loved debate and democracy.

Odysseus stood for everything Ajax despised. Odysseus's qualities were ascendant. Ajax had become an anachronism. Sophocles, with his remarkable insight into human character, revealed the inner workings of Ajax's psyche. When Achilles' armor was denied Ajax and given instead to the craftier, less heroic Odysseus, the affront so rankled Ajax that he decided on a plan of revenge that entailed the murder of the Greek leaders. But the goddess Athena intervened and turned him instead

on the Greeks' sheep and oxen. Believing them to be his enemies, he slaughtered them in the night. When he came to his
senses the next day amid the blood and gore, he was so overcome with grief and shame that he killed himself.

PRIDE GOETH BEFORE A MANAGERIAL FALL

Ajax's crime was not that he had slaughtered a few livestock.
Nor was it even that he wanted to take revenge on his unap-
preciative bosses. Ajax's real offense was that all-too-frequent
product of success—excessive pride. Early in the tale, Sophocles relates a prophetic story of the youthful Ajax, leaving his
home on the island of Salamis to join the Greek army. His
father offered him some parting advice: "My son," he said, "seek
victory in arms, but seek it always with the help of heaven."
Ajax answered haughtily, "Father, with the help of gods even a
weak man might win, but I, even without their aid, trust to
bring glory within my grasp." This was perhaps excusable
youthful arrogance. But as an adult, Ajax bragged of his
omnipotence directly to the goddess Athena. This was unpardonable. From that moment on, Athena—once his ally—engineered his downfall.

It's an ancient story that is really chillingly modern, one that
struck close to home when the Challenger space shuttle
exploded in 1986. The central element in the disaster was not,
as most believed, a flawed seal in the shuttle's booster rocket. It
was excessive pride. NASA was blinded, according to the *New
York Times*, by pride in its past achievements, dazzled by its

record of success. After all, it had sent humans into space fifty-five times without loss of life, and it had even landed men on the moon safely. The resulting cover-up and complacency turned the world's most advanced space program into a Greek tragedy.[1]

Ajax is a tragedy of pride leading inevitably to a fall. Ajax's arrogance not only offended the gods but also blinded him—as it can any manager—to what was changing in the organizational world around him. Unable to read this organizational change, he could not adapt. It is a tale frequently repeated in modern organizations—a tale of a supersuccessful company so certain of its success and contemptuous of its competitors that it fails to notice that its market is changing. By the time its leaders do notice, it is invariably too late.

FAILURE TO ADAPT IN FAST FOOD AND HIGH TECH

That is exactly what happened at McDonald's, where a misplaced sense of pride and the inability to realize what customers and franchisees wanted engineered the company's decline in revenue and slide from the preeminent position in the fast-food industry. While competitors introduced new and innovative fare, McDonald's remained wedded to a menu that was old and tired. Even attempts to attract new customers were fundamentally flawed; its new line of Arch Deluxe sandwiches intended to appeal to adults, for example, was basically a rerun of its same old offerings. And customers noticed. The line was a flop. Yet, even then, executives' inability to admit they made a mistake had McDonald's Michael Quinlan proclaiming that the line had "exceeded expectations."[2]

Hubris also led to bad judgment and terrible management at Silicon Graphics Inc. The computer maker that rose to unexpected heights in a few short years with its powerful computer-animated graphics (used in the film *Jurassic Park*, for example) became so enamored with its success that executives forgot to pay attention to what was going on around them. While competitors were aggressively courting the personal-computer market by producing more powerful workstations that could compete with SGI's, company executives were so caught up in their success that they disdained such mundane business practices as inventory and quality control. Instead, they turned their attention to more sexy challenges such as interactive cable TV and supercomputers, ignoring the business of selling computers that led to SGI's fame in the first place. Customers, disenchanted with unmet delivery schedules, numerous breakdowns, and lack of attention to their needs, began to go elsewhere. They now had alternatives.

At the same time, CEO Edward R. McCracken's involvement as cochair of President Clinton's National Information Infrastructure Advisory Council left a dearth of leadership at SGI. Opportunities to expand its initial entry into the Internet were ignored, costing SGI its place as a front-runner on the Net. Valued key executives, frustrated by the lack of direction at SGI, left in record numbers, often to join or start up businesses that are now fierce competitors to their former employer. Quarter after quarter of lower-than-expected revenues, plummeting stock values, and loss of market share in the workstation market left SGI scrambling to hold on to even a piece of its former glory. Conceded McCracken: "If we can't produce good quarters, we're not going to have a future."[3]

The leaders at McDonald's and Silicon Graphics might have fared better if they had read Sophocles' *Ajax*. It is an invaluable story for managers: ambition, the desire to succeed, and a tendency to believe that good fortune is permanent can lead them to repeat the mistakes, if not the tragedy, of Ajax.

Antigone
The Dangers of Dogged Persistence

One of the Greeks' most urgent and perplexing questions, as they looked at the tension between individuals and organizations, was the difference between "natural" and "man-made" law. They wondered whether people's essential nature differed from that imposed on them by habit and custom, those superficial coverings with which society—as well as many large organizations—envelops and sometimes suffocates the individual. How might this affect leadership? What should a leader do, for example, when a member of the organization challenges its rules and policies?

Sophocles' tragedy *Antigone* grapples with these knotty questions. Written almost 2,500 years ago, it was an immediate success. But it is a very modern story about the conflict between individual and organization, the responsibilities of those who lead, and the high cost of inflexibility. The play's name (one meaning of "Antigone" is "born to oppose") unmistakably suggests the power struggle between two strong-willed people that animates the play.

A STORY OF ONE WOMAN'S CHALLENGE
TO THE ORGANIZATION

At the beginning of the story, two young soldiers had been killed in combat outside the walls of Thebes, a city in ancient Greece. Creon, the Theban ruler, decreed that one of them was to be given full burial rites. The other, Polyneices (who had attacked the city), was to be left unburied and unlamented, a fate that the Greeks believed would eternally condemn the soul. Anyone who violated this order was to be punished by death. Antigone, the heroine of the play, disregarded Creon's order and buried Polyneices, even though she knew this meant treason. Uncompromising even though she understood the consequences, she chose to obey the "laws of gods" instead of the "laws of man." When Creon learned that Polyneices had received the proper burial rites, he ordered the body uncovered and the offender arrested. It turned out to be Antigone.

After she was apprehended, Creon's son, Haemon—who was betrothed to Antigone—pleaded with his father to show mercy. Haemon argued with Creon, reminding him that public sentiment was strongly in favor of reducing the punishment. But the autocratic Creon would have none of it. He ordered Antigone thrown into a cave where she was to die. At this point, the prophet of the city, articulating the will of the gods, told Creon that his son would die if he did not relent and provide a proper burial for the dead warrior. Finally, Creon reversed his decision, ordered the burial, and raced off to release Antigone. He arrived too late, for Antigone had killed herself, as had his wife and son. In an unforgettable closing scene, we see Creon devastated and desolate, prey to his own unstinting absolutism.

CREON: DECISION MAKER EXTRAORDINAIRE

It would be too simple to accuse Creon of wrongheaded leadership. After all, he believed he was doing what was best for his organization. The facts of the case were clear: Polyneices *was* a traitor. Antigone *had* flagrantly violated the rules. Creon was a conscientious leader, concerned—above all else—with preserving his organization and maintaining his position of power. He was decisive, as is appropriate for a leader, and he understood the importance of strong, uncompromising leadership:

> There is no greater wrong than disobedience.
> This ruins cities, this tears down our homes,
> this breaks the battlefront in panic-rout.
> If men live decently it is because
> discipline saves their very lives for them.

Early in the play, as Creon enters in full armor with a military escort, the chorus leader sings:

> Now here he comes, the king of the land,
> Creon, Menoeceus's son,
> newly named by the gods' new fate.

What plan that beats about his mind
has made him call this council-session,
sending his summons to all?

Creon's eloquent reply would, with only minor modifica-
tions, sound like that of any contemporary leader who has succeeded in stabilizing a troubled organization:

My friends, the very gods who shook the state
with mighty surge have set it straight again.

THE ORGANIZATION CHALLENGED

But this stability was not to last long, for Antigone had defied
the rules of the organization. Creon faced the kind of situation
that leaders frequently face, a choice between recognizing the
dictates of the individual and the rules and regulations of the
organization:

Since I have caught her in the open act,
the only one in town who disobeyed, I
shall not now proclaim myself a liar,
but kill her. . . .
If I allow disorder in my house
I'd surely have to license it abroad.
A man who deals in fairness with his own,
he can make manifest justice in the state.
But he who crosses the law, or forces it,
or hopes to bring the rulers under him,
shall never have a word of praise from me.

The man the state has put in place must have
obedient hearing to his least command
when it is right, and even when it's not.

Haemon—motivated by his love for both Antigone and
Creon—made things even more difficult. He pleaded with
Creon to relent:

Then, do not have one mind, and one alone
that only your opinion can be right.
Whoever thinks that he alone is wise,
his eloquence, his mind, above the rest,
come the unfolding, shows his emptiness.
A man, though wise, should never be ashamed
of learning more, and must unbend his mind.
No, yield your wrath, allow a change of stand.
Young as I am, if I may give advice,
I'd say it would be best if men were born
perfect in wisdom, but that failing this
(which often fails) it can be no dishonor
to learn from others when they speak good sense.

Creon was unimpressed with his son's argument. He ordered
Antigone to be executed. In her defense, she argued that there
was a profound difference between natural law and Creon's
man-made law. She broke the latter law, she says, because:

For me it was not Zeus who made that order.
Nor did that justice who lives with the gods below
mark out such laws to hold among mankind.

> Nor did I think your orders were so strong
> · that you, a mortal man, could overrun
> the gods' unwritten and unfailing laws.
> Not now, nor yesterday's; they always live.

For Creon's harsh treatment of Antigone, history has labeled him—perhaps with good reason—a tyrant and autocrat, a leader whose only real interest was obedience to power and the pursuit of absolute rule. Without question, his was a flawed leadership. Nevertheless, Creon's fundamental predicament— that of choosing between the good of the individual and what he saw as the good of the organization—must strike a familiar chord to all who lead. Resolving this dilemma is perhaps the ultimate test of the leader, ancient or modern.

Antigone is also the tale of a leader who allows tenacity— that rare ability to persevere against overwhelming odds—to turn into *downright stubbornness*. Creon's greatest flaw, it turns out, was not his dictatorial style of leadership but his towering inflexibility and his unwillingness to listen to another side. He did not change his decision until a trusted prophet told him that his state was "sick" and that his autocratic leadership principles were wrongheaded, and predicted that his son would die if Antigone were executed. By then it was too late. Antigone, his son, and his wife were dead.

THE PROBLEM AT FORD

Tenacity transformed into sheer stubbornness is not limited to the ancient Greeks. It is a thoroughly modern phenomenon.

Consider the case of Henry Ford, the industrial miracle-worker who achieved, shortly after World War I, phenomenal growth and seemingly limitless efficiency in automobile production. Ford began with a remarkably simple idea: build an inexpensive car—the renowned Model T—for a large public. His mission: to produce more cars per day at ever-decreasing unit costs. With the monomaniacal zeal so common among entrepreneurs, Ford concentrated on this one truly "big idea," producing thousands of cars that would "get you there and get you back." There is no doubt that his single-mindedness paid off wonderfully. For fifteen years, the Ford Motor Company was on an unprecedented "roll," achieving a whopping 66 percent share and unchallenged leadership of the American automobile market.

But then the Ford success story was over, an ironic victim of the same single-mindedness that had accounted for the company's early growth. When consumer preference shifted to comfort, styling, and performance, the Model T became an anachronism. Like Creon, Henry Ford did not listen to his advisers until it was too late. William Knudsen, for one, left the company in 1921 because he could not persuade his boss to make a model change. He went on to head General Motors's supersuccessful Chevrolet Division and destroy Ford's lead in the low-priced segment of the auto market. Ford's inflexibility, coupled with his astounding absolutism (he employed a secret police force and exercised the tightest of centralized control), nearly bankrupted his company in the 1920s, when its market share plummeted to a paltry 20 percent and GM took over first place.

KNOWING WHEN TO PULL THE PLUG

Recognizing that Creon-like persistence can sometimes be bad for the bottom line may be a bitter pill to swallow but good medicine. Executives at Commerce Clearing House (CCH) seem to have learned this lesson. In the late 1980s, publisher CCH was a firmly established supplier of reports for accounting and law firms, corporations, and government agencies, and had the third-highest return on equity among twenty-two U.S. publishers. But then things began to change. While the company held doggedly to its mainframe computer system and providing information in print to its customers, the customers were turning to PCs and electronic databases for the same information. CCH's revenue plummeted. Noted Oakleigh Thorne, executive vice president of CCH, "It's like we were sitting there with our feet stuck in concrete. We were so wedded to the great revenue we were getting, we didn't have the courage to migrate to being a PC software company." CCH did find the courage, however, to admit that sticking to its print legacy was a grave mistake and engineered a dramatic move—a shift to electronic publishing—to regain its customers.[4]

THE ART OF COMPROMISE

The crucial point to be learned from *Antigone* is that leadership is the art of compromise. The story is a tragedy because the two principal characters were unwilling to negotiate, unwilling to compromise. The result was disastrous for them and for their organization.

The story of Creon and of the tragic consequences that his intransigent leadership produced is far from ancient. That story is lived out today with remarkable frequency. And just as Creon failed when he confused stubbornness with good leadership, so too can modern leaders. Henry Ford, a real asset to his company in its early stages of growth, almost destroyed his maturing enterprise because of his dogged persistence. The leaders of Commerce Clearing House were more willing to be flexible and admit errors. Unlike Creon, they took a hit, admitted they'd made a mistake, and put it behind them.

PART TWO

THE RENAISSANCE

Triumph of Individual over Organization

The Greeks tried to balance the needs of individuals and organizations. In contrast, the Renaissance glorified the individual—subjugating the organization when necessary to accommodate personal needs and aspirations. The individual transcended the organization. Man knew no limits. This attitude often stimulated unprecedented discovery, conquest, and learning. Sometimes it fed individual greed. But always the Renaissance gave new scope to human potential, revealing the simple truth that individuals are more important than organizations—and sometimes more powerful.

In this part, the great writings of the Renaissance serve as a microscope through which we can view the potentials, the frailties, the victories, and the tragedies of the fascinating "universal men" of the period as they struggled to manage their lives, their organizations, and their destinies. The author's gallery of unforgettable characters in *The Canterbury Tales*, a work of the late Middle Ages, presages the Renaissance's interest in each person's remarkable individuality. In this work, Chaucer demonstrates convincingly that it is the height of folly to pigeonhole people, as so many modern management theories do. Renaissance man was, after all, unique, much too individualistic to be successfully stereotyped. Baldassare Castiglione's *Book of the Courtier* provides leaders of any age with a philosophy of behavior. It carried the customs of the Italian Renaissance north to Britain more than 400 years ago, and today it illuminates our understanding of the style with which leaders lead. Machiavelli's treatise *The Prince* explores yet another aspect of the Renaissance, the cult of virtue, a creed that exhorted every man to be great, even if this meant setting himself above all ethical and religious training and relying only on intrigue and frightening boldness. *The Prince*—for better or worse—made traditional morality obsolete. In *King Lear*, Shakespeare examines an aging executive's unwillingness to release the long-held reins of power and his flawed delegation and succession plans. In *Macbeth*, Shakespeare portrays the effects of unbridled ambition that seeks only personal gain. *Othello* demonstrates what happens when a leader loses faith in his intuition and allows himself to be manipulated by another.

Renaissance Man as Entrepreneur Prototype

If there is a forerunner of the individualistic, freewheeling, charismatic mavericks we call entrepreneurs—those rare individuals who regularly accomplish alone what giant organizations have not even dreamed of—it is Renaissance man. Like his modern counterpart, he was a daring visionary whose uncanny ability to rise above the limits and confines of "his" organization—the church and the state—enabled him to change the world. Renaissance man put himself, his reputation, and his fortune at risk long before Fred Smith created Federal Express, Henry Ford built his Model T, or Eli Whitney invented the cotton gin.

It is difficult to date precisely when Renaissance man—and his era—appeared. But most scholars agree that what we call "the Renaissance" took root in fourteenth-century Italy, then crept gradually and deliberately toward northern Europe over the next three or four centuries. No single date marks its beginning or end. The Renaissance was not an event; it was a *state of mind* in which one feature stands out: the celebration of the individual over the organization.

The Power of the Individual

Although Renaissance man read Greek and Roman texts with great interest, he never embraced the goal of balance between individual and organization that had so enthused the ancients. Pericles' *Funeral Oration*, declaring that every Athenian was equally a private and public citizen and that individual and organizational goals must converge, would have been thoroughly out of place in the Renaissance. Instead of seeking an integration of the individual and the organization, Renaissance man attempted to gain permanent release from the confining yoke of the organization. As soon as he discovered his limitless capabilities, he sought to achieve success and fame, to amass wealth, to exert power; these became the *sine qua non* of the Renaissance.

Time and time again, Renaissance man changed his institutions and challenged commonly held beliefs. Henry VIII defied the church in Rome, weakening the Catholic establishment for all time. Galileo upset the religious and scientific establishments by inventing an instrument to study the heavenly order. Machiavelli, in legitimizing the use of power in pursuit of individual gain, encouraged the hostile takeover of existing regimes. And in *The Last Supper*, Leonardo da Vinci departed dramatically from previous interpretations by placing Judas among the apostles.

Emerging from the Middle Ages

Understanding how this dramatic change in man's relationship to his institutions took place requires a brief look at the period that preceded the Renaissance. In the Middle Ages, man was conscious of himself only as a member of an organization—church, race, people, or family. He was submerged in society, and his first concern tended to be its good, not his individual welfare. The church was the all-encompassing medieval organization, omnipotent and omnipresent, supported by leaders whose "divine right" brooked no resistance. There was a highly stratified society with little mobility, and a culture that, instead of rewarding self-reliance, punished it as a sign of arrogance.

Emerging from this gloomy backdrop came Renaissance man, an individualist, a "humanist," who placed a new emphasis on himself and his place in the universe. He revived classical antiquity (relying greatly, it must be noted, on the patient work of medieval copyists who preserved many of the ancient texts). He engaged in geographic discoveries that changed his world dramatically. He conceived of marvelous mechanical contraptions that anticipated much of what we think of as "modern," including helicopters and space flight. He learned that power was as much a function of individual ability as it was of legitimate authority. In marked contrast to the ancient Greek commitment to the power of reason, Renaissance man celebrated the power of will. Petrarch, the fourteenth-century Italian poet and classical scholar who became known as the "father of the Renaissance," put it well: "It is better to will the good," he said, "than to know the truth." Not surprisingly, Renaissance man worshiped a kind of virtue that valued ambition and fame over goodness and morality. When he invented capitalism and banking, Renaissance man became truly independent. He was, indeed, the first entrepreneur, relying not on religion or organization or any outside force for guidance, but exclusively on his remarkable savvy, wile, and talent.

As the Renaissance idea of individualism caught on, it was reflected in art, poetry, drama, and philosophy. In art, paintings, sculptures, and drawings focused on the human anatomy in great detail. The works of Leonardo da Vinci broke new ground by glorifying the power and ability of the individual. Other artists concentrated on rendering, in the minutest detail, the faces of their subjects, intending to show joy, suffering, or some other depth of an individual's character. In poetry, there was a new interest in romantic love between man and woman. In drama, the Renaissance gave us Shakespeare. His thirty-seven plays delve much more into the motives, potentials, and tragedies of individuals than into the rise or fall of organizations. Shakespeare cared little about what happened to Denmark; he was fascinated with the character of Hamlet. Likewise, his analysis of the tragic decline of King Lear left little room for an examination of Lear's kingdom. And the audience dwelt on and identified with Lear, not his realm. The most fascinating thing about the Renaissance is its focus on the individual. That is what makes its literature so valuable for leaders of any age.

SIX

CHAUCER

Those Annoying Little Differences

Like pilots whose navigational systems sometimes fail, leaders fly blind with alarming frequency. Although leadership theory abounds (one book summarizes more than 3,000 studies), much of it is based on a fetchingly simple—but dangerously flawed—premise. Human beings, it postulates, are like chessmen or tin soldiers. They can be relied on to move in predictable ways, responding to outside stimuli much like Pavlov's salivating dogs. But the theorists have failed to take into account an essential part of man's humanness: his penchant for maddening inconsistency. They hate to face the troubling fact that unlike the phenomena of chemistry or physics—where water always boils at 212 degrees Fahrenheit—humans often behave in unexpected ways. No wonder that Harold Geneen, onetime head of ITT, charged—with stinging accuracy—that much of what passes for leadership and management theories is like the paper hoops used by circus clowns, which look solid until someone jumps through them.[1]

Have You Heard the Latest One About Leadership?

These theories are often built on the shakiest of intellectual foundations: dichotomy and stereotype. There is, for example, the theory that posits a Theory X–Theory Y dichotomy. Arguably *the* most popular leadership theory over the past twenty years, it is glowingly described in every major management text and eagerly touted in countless executive-training programs. Its message is simple: Most managers (the "Theory X" ones) think their workers are drones, incapable of assuming responsibility and anything more than minimal effort; other managers (the "Theory Y" types) view their employees as near-perfect winners, office dynamos full of selfless dedication to the organization. Pygmalion, the legendary Greek king, is said to have influenced the behavior of those around him simply by communicating his expectations. This theory breezily asserts that if leaders would just, like Pygmalion, "become more Theory Y," so would their workers. The theory plays remarkably well in the classroom and the corporate seminar room. But it is so user-friendly that it is practically useless. *Real* people, unlike simplified theoretical constructs, are anything but binary, "either-or" beings. They are infinitely complex. The point is that reductionist leadership theories don't work: people cannot be stereotyped and neatly categorized. They don't "dichotomize" easily.

A Keen Observer of Human Uniqueness

The most discriminating and deeply felt observations of man's uniqueness have always come from artists and writers. A painting by Brueghel, a story by Mark Twain, a Shakespeare performance by Olivier—all serve to remind us of the unpredictable psychic twists and turns that make one person's nature remarkably different from another's. But few in history have appreciated man's multifaceted and unpredictable character as much, or communicated it so well, as the fourteenth-century English poet Geoffrey Chaucer. Chaucer was a genial and urbane man whose wry sense of humor surfaced in everything he wrote. Portly, of ruddy complexion, and equipped with a drooping mustache, he looked every bit like the good storyteller he was. In the seventeenth century, John Dryden, himself one of England's greatest poets, called Chaucer the "father of English poetry." Chaucer was to the English what Homer was to the Greeks.

He was born in 1340. The Middle Ages and its overarching belief that the community is more important than the individual was nearing its end. In its place, the Renaissance was soon to assert a new and profound belief in the individual.

Chaucer missed none of this. He was a dedicated observer of human nature, able to see both its humor and its tragedy. Uncommonly intrigued by human frailties, he tried to discover the secrets of human motivation and the "good life." In this he was helped greatly by a superb education and the lifelong support of the English court. He was a thinker as well as a doer, both a poet and a civil servant. He applied himself daily to affairs of state and business, but he never failed to bury himself in books at night. He served three kings as courtier, diplomatic errand-runner, and customs official—a career that must have been useful in developing keen observation and a deep understanding of human nature.

The best-known product of Chaucer's genius is his masterpiece, *The Canterbury Tales*. Hugely popular since it was first published, this collection of stories, mostly in verse, is full of charmingly entertaining looks at man's relationship to man, at man's virtues and his vices. Chaucer's good humor pervades it, making the consideration of its sometimes-weighty questions unusually palatable. But above all, *The Canterbury Tales* demonstrates Chaucer's awesome ability to create memorable characters—warts and all. Because of their universality, these characters are at home in any age. And they are, without exception, real people—complex rather than one-dimensional. Together they form what has been rightly called "the greatest portrait gallery in English literature."

The tale begins as a group of pilgrims—including Chaucer (who served as the narrator)—gathered at the Tabard Inn, near London, to begin a journey to Canterbury Cathedral. It was a remarkably varied bunch, including a distinguished knight, a womanizing squire, a jolly fat monk, a money-loving friar, a successful merchant, a diseased cook, a God-fearing tenant farmer, a bagpipe-playing miller, and the host. At his suggestion, they agreed to engage in a storytelling contest en route, the winner of which would receive a free dinner on their return. Although the stories themselves (the tales) make delightful reading, it is in the prologue that Chaucer described his fellow travelers in meticulous detail.

The Danger of Stereotypes

The "Wife of Bath"—the richest and most well rounded of Chaucer's characters—was a gaudy, lower-middle-class weaver from near the town of Bath. She was gap-toothed and ruddy, as comfortable on a horse as in a carriage. She laughed easily and loved good jokes, which she frequently told. And she was elaborately overdressed, unremittingly aggressive, and slightly deaf:

> A worthy woman from beside Bath city
> Was with us, somewhat deaf, which was a pity.
> In making cloth she showed so great a bent
> She bettered those of Ypres and of Ghent.
> In all the parish not a dame dared stir
> Towards the altar steps in front of her,
> And if indeed they did, so wrath was she
> As to be quite put out of charity.
> Her kerchiefs were of finely woven ground;
> I dared have sworn they weighed a good ten pound,
> The ones she wore on Sunday, on her head.

Marriage was her *real* occupation, and she claimed abundant expertise in it. After all, she had had five husbands:

> "If there were no authority on earth
> Except experience, mine, for what it's worth,
> And that's enough for me, all goes to show
> That marriage is a misery and a woe;

For let me say, if I may make so bold,
My lords, since when I was but twelve years old,
Thanks be to God Eternal evermore,
Five husbands have I had at the church door."

She was understandably dogmatic about marriage, insisting
that women should do as she did: always have the upper hand.
Chattering away in her gossipy manner, she regaled her fellow
travelers—most of whom were men—with frank advice on
love, sex, marriage, and even medieval economics:

"Now of my fifth, last husband let me tell.
God never let his soul be sent to Hell!
And yet he was my worst, and many a blow
He struck me still can ache along my row
Of ribs, and will until my dying day.
But in our bed he was so fresh and gay,
So coaxing, so persuasive . . . Heaven knows
Whenever he wanted it—my *belle chose*—
Though he had beaten me in every bone
He still could wheedle me to love, I own.
I think I loved him best, I'll tell no lie.
He was disdainful in his love, that's why.
We women have a curious fantasy
In such affairs, or so it seems to me.
When something's difficult, or can't be had,
We crave and cry for it all day like mad.
Forbid a thing, we pine for it all night,
Press fast upon us and we take to flight,

We use disdain in offering our wares.
A throng of buyers sends prices up at fairs,
Cheap goods have little value, they suppose;
And that's a thing that every woman knows."

Yet, the tale that this apparently crude and brash woman tells next reveals a paradox. Expecting a robust and realistic story, the reader gets a fairy tale instead. Full of nostalgia, her tale is a poignant love story in which an aging hag is turned into a beautiful girl, finds a young and handsome husband, and lives happily ever after. Underneath the coarse exterior of the Wife of Bath, there is a beguilingly gentle and refined woman. It is this incongruity that makes her such an appealing and realistic character. She is full of surprises and paradoxes, incapable of being classified, sorted, or neatly pigeonholed; she is human.

So it is with Chaucer's other pilgrims. The apparently successful merchant, it turns out, is deeply in debt:

There was a merchant with a forking beard
And motley dress; high on his horse he sat,
Upon his head a Flemish beaver hat
And on his feet daintily buckled boots.
He told of his opinions and pursuits
In solemn tones. He harped on his increase
Of capital; there should be sea-police
(He thought) upon the Harwich-Holland ranges;
He was expert in dabbling in exchanges.
This estimable merchant so had set
His wits to work, none knew he was in debt.

> He was so stately in administration,
> In loans and bargains and negotiation.
> He was an excellent fellow all the same.
> To tell the truth I do not know his name.

The merchant gave the appearance of wealth (the beaver hat, the buckled boots) and at the same time showed a lack of interest in his appearance (the motley dress). He was opinionated, but "an excellent fellow all the same." He was a good trader, but in debt. The merchant, like the Wife of Bath, defies simple categorization.

Yet another example of Chaucer's ability to portray the paradoxes within individuals is his description of the manciple, or purchasing agent:

> The manciple came from the inner temple;
> All caterers might follow his example
> In buying victuals; he was never rash
> Whether he bought on credit or paid cash.
> He used to watch the market most precisely
> And got in first, and so he did quite nicely.
> Now isn't it a marvel of God's grace
> That an illiterate fellow can outpace
> The wisdom of a heap of learned men?

Chaucer's purchasing agent, it turns out, was brighter and more skilled than most of the thirty lawyers he served. He was excellent in his job, yet he was illiterate. He had no business being that good at his job. Chaucer's genius, however, is that he did not allow his characters to be stereotyped. He presented a view of the individual that defies easy labeling.

Human Chameleons

The intriguing group of characters that Geoffrey Chaucer assembled in *The Canterbury Tales* provides an excellent reminder that people are complex, not one-dimensional. Each individual is—as psychologist Leona Tyler points out—a "collection of selves," capable of being a different person at different times. According to Tyler, we are as mutable as chameleons, those tiny animals that rapidly change the color of their skin.[2]

Take George Foreman, for example. In a former life, he turned his street-kid toughness from juvenile delinquency to boxing: at age twenty, he won an Olympic gold medal; five years later, he knocked out Joe Frazier to become heavyweight champion of the world, a title he held until losing to Muhammad Ali in 1974. By all accounts, his success in the ring didn't change his street-tough attitude outside the ring, however. Described as "rude, mean, and uncooperative," the often-sullen Foreman was definitely not on anyone's best-loved list. Yet, today he is a well-loved American icon whose face and voice—along with his idiosyncratic decision to name each of his five sons George—are familiar to millions.

Foreman's transformation from unlikely hero to national folk hero is a powerful example of the danger of stereotyping people. When Foreman engineered a boxing comeback in the late '80s, he was no longer the nasty young man people remembered. He was courteous, he was likeable—he had panache—

and although he lost his bid in 1991 to regain the heavyweight title, he won enormous respect for the way he handled himself. Evidencing a natural wit and charm that few, if any, would have suspected he possessed twenty years earlier, Foreman was soon in demand on the talk-show circuit. His deprecating humor as spokesperson for Salton-Maxin's Lean, Mean, Fat-Reducing Grilling Machine and as a commentator for HBO's televised fights added to his fame, as did his stint on the sitcom *George*, in which he played an ex-fighter who ran an after-school program for troubled high school kids. The sitcom was art imitating life—Foreman had already used income from his return to boxing to establish the George Foreman Youth and Community Center in Houston, a facility designed to help troubled kids.[3]

Foreman is not unusual. Paradoxes, of course, are what make people as well as Chaucer's imaginary characters so fascinatingly human—and productive. The unlikeliest people, for example, have invented some remarkably successful products. Imagine how Chaucer would have described King Gillette, the lowly traveling cork salesman who invented the safety razor. Or the two musicians who invented Kodachrome film. Or the patent attorney who discovered xerography, the undertaker who created automatic telephone dialing, and the veterinarian who originated the pneumatic tire.[4]

The central point to be learned from Chaucer is that people can't be stereotyped. Pigeonholing, labeling, or otherwise categorizing people according to the latest leadership theory can cause you to miss some important hidden potentials. The person you view as the office ne'er-do-well may be the organization's next wildly successful fast-tracker.

SEVEN

CASTIGLIONE

More than a Renaissance "Miss Manners"

Falling in love with the quick fix has become a habit among American managers. Why else would such a surprisingly large number of them embrace so eagerly, and with so much apparent gullibility, every new fad and fashion that comes along? This uniquely American affinity for managerial avant-garde has resulted in a series of leadership crazes rivaling the hula hoop and sack dresses. Take "portfolio management," for example. This gimmick transformed perfectly normal companies into "stars," "question marks," "cash cows," and "dogs." The idea was intriguingly simple. Use market growth and share data to identify winning and losing product lines or divisions. Then sit back and manage them as a stockbroker runs a client's portfolio, balancing risk against reward, culling out the dregs, investing in the highfliers. But it didn't work. Portfolio management enthusiasts forgot the basics. They didn't nose around the factory. They stopped listening to their customers. And they forgot the basic challenge they faced: creating value. Managing a company as if it were nothing more than a basketful of stocks and bonds turned out to be a theorist's dream but a practicing manager's nightmare.

Then there was "matrix management." Hundreds of perfectly normal companies reorganized themselves into rows and columns that looked vaguely like neat military formations. The goal was to establish specialist "hit teams" that could be quickly deployed throughout the organization as needed, returning temporarily to home base when their tasks were completed. There was one big problem: no one knew to whom to report. The resulting chaos made the matrix one of management's shortest, and most confusing, fads. The list of glitzy panaceas that don't work could go on and on. (Remember scientific management, T-groups, sensitivity training, management by objectives, one-minute managing, zero-based budgeting, and PERT, for example?)

But the crazes keep coming. A recent one is executive etiquette. Based on the simple premise that good manners may have a lot more to do with career success than does the bottom line, nearly everyone has gotten into the act. Even normally down-to-business business schools now offer courses ranging from dining habits to Internet protocol. Howard University, for example, offers business students seminars on such topics as art appreciation, telephone etiquette, and table manners. Charlie E. Mahone Jr., chairman of the department of finance, international business, and insurance, said the seminars are important because not all students know the niceties of etiquette.[1]

Joanne Mahanes, career development coordinator at the University of Virginia's College of Arts and Sciences, tells of a student who salted his food before tasting it during a lunch interview: he didn't receive a job offer because the recruiter saw this as a sign of a hasty decision maker.[2]

While this may seem extreme, remember that perception is in the eye of the beholder. And according to Ann Marie Sabath, it's hard for individuals to climb the ladder of success if bosses and clients don't perceive them as looking and acting the part. Sabath, founder of At Ease Inc., a Cincinnati firm that offers corporate etiquette training, is one of a spate of updated Emily Posts who tell you everything you want to know—and much you don't—about workplace politesse. They offer handy tips on everything from elevator etiquette, to workplace discretion, to what not to order during a business dinner. And even etiquette-wise executives may need a refresher course now and again, as changing technology and global markets create new issues such as voice mail and E-mail etiquette and cultural protocol.[3]

Ancient Advice on Managing with Good Manners

As with corporate culture, however, there's considerably more than hype to the contemporary concern about courtesy, manners, and style. Such concerns have a long and venerable history. In fact, the oldest book in the world, a dusty Egyptian papyrus, contains advice from an Egyptian father to his son on polite conduct. The Proverbs of Solomon provide shrewd and pithy counsel on personal conduct, as does *Works and Days*, the rambling poem of the ancient Greek Hesiod. Shakespeare dispenses literature's most unforgettable tips on good manners when—in *Hamlet*—Polonius says to his departing son:

> Give every man thy ear, but few thy voice;
> Take each man's censure, but reserve thy judgment.
> Costly thy habit as thy purse can buy,
> But not express'd in fancy; rich, not gaudy;
> For the apparel oft proclaims the man,
> And they in France of the best rank and station
> Are of a most select and generous chief in that.
> Neither a borrower nor a lender be;
> For loan oft loses both itself and friend,
> And borrowing dulls the edge of husbandry.
> This above all: to thine own self be true,
> And it must follow, as the night the day,
> Thou canst not then be false to any man.

One classic, however, truly stands out. It is *The Book of the Courtier*. Published in 1528, at the height of the Renaissance, it was the first book to focus entirely on the topic of politeness and the cultivation of the true gentleman. Its author, Baldassare Castiglione, was himself a man of impeccable manners, a "courtier" who learned the subtle art of chivalry at the court of the duke of Urbino in northern Italy. As a youth, he was educated in the refinements of society. Later he served his duke as a soldier, diplomat, and adviser. In his old age, he turned to the priesthood and very nearly became a cardinal. Through it all, he never failed to make quite an impression on those he served. When Castiglione died in 1529, Charles V, the Holy Roman emperor, eulogized him as "one of the greatest gentlemen in the world."

Samuel Johnson, doyen of eighteenth-century London literary society, pronounced *The Book of the Courtier* "the best thing ever written on good breeding." Harold Nicolson, whose slim 1969 volume *Good Behavior* examines everything from bird-handling etiquette to Petronius's satirical advice on handling bores, describes it as "the most influential manual on deportment and courtly behavior ever published." Castiglione's masterpiece reflects that fundamental Renaissance trait, a striving for the finest possible human personality and culture. And, like most other classics, it is still highly practical for anyone who seeks to lead. For Renaissance men, what mattered most were the guidelines for good conduct that they could glean from Castiglione's book. British gentlemen, in particular, rushed to purchase translations and quickly emulated the fashionable behavior it described. Many returned from their tours abroad acting, doubtless with great hilarity, more like Bolognese than like the Yorkshiremen they really were.

More than Just a "Courtesy Book"

The story begins in the winter of 1507, when the court of Urbino had just hosted a visit from the pope. A group of dignitaries, including scholars, church officials, artists, soldiers, and diplomats, remained behind at the castle. Their discussion

of the characteristics, duties, and accomplishments of the
ideal courtier provides a remarkable look at the anatomy of
leadership.

There is more to this book than instant sixteenth-century
culture—something in addition to detailed instructions on
bowing, genuflecting, and walking backward. As in the Renaissance court, just to survive, many a modern organization leader
needs all of the diplomatic guile that he or she can muster. For
better or worse, the near-aristocracies of the contemporary corporation sometimes echo those of the sixteenth-century court.
In this sense, *The Book of the Courtier* is as relevant to modern
leaders as it was to Renaissance nobles. More important, Castiglione's book did not simply present a list of terse rules for
mannerly behavior. Written in the form of Socratic dialectic, it
offers the reader nothing less than a philosophy of good behavior and social interaction. The author, mercifully, is far more
interested in scrutinizing human behavior in all of its subtle
complexities than in offering specific rules for success. For
example, when Castiglione urges the courtier to wear dark-
colored clothing, he analyzes the psychological effects that col-
ors have on others and the image they project.

Such thinking might explain IBM's once-famous dress code,
which although unwritten, might as well have been chiseled in
stone. At one time, IBMers *did* religiously wear dark conservative
suits, white shirts, and subdued ties. And even their technicians
looked more like bankers than repairmen. As did Castiglione
before him, Tom Watson Sr., IBM's founder, analyzed the psychology of appearance. His conclusion? Dressing conservatively
consistently results in better treatment by the customer.

The Importance of a Flexible Response

Another thing that separates *The Book of the Courtier* from mere courtesy manuals is a refreshing absence of dogmatism. The dialectic form leaves no room for it and encourages instead energetic debate and a frequently uncomfortable sense of uncertainty. Every thesis is closely followed by an antithesis. One character's notion of the ideal courtier is not another's. What works in one situation may fail miserably in another. The successful courtier, concludes Castiglione, must be capable of responding flexibly to each situation. Like Proteus, the Greek sea-god who could change his form or appearance at will, the courtier must be capable of lightning-quick role changes. In this sense, too, Castiglione's ideal courtier looks strikingly like the modern corporate leaders whose roles must shift countless times each day—from scrapping with union leaders in the morning, to cheerleading the sales force over lunch, to cajoling bankers in the afternoon, to hobnobbing with major stockholders in the evening. Theirs is a world of uncertainty and chance, just like Castiglione's. *The Book of the Courtier* is his effort to show leaders how to cope with that world with dignity, integrity, and style.

Sprezzatura—Making It All Seem Easy

J. Pierpont Finch, the hugely ambitious character in the hit Broadway musical *How to Succeed in Business Without Really Trying*, was the dynamo who rose from the mail room to the executive suite simply by showing the boss how hard he worked.

Castiglione would have felt that Finch—and all other two-briefcase-toting workaholics—had it all wrong. Real class, he claimed, consists of making the difficult look easy. What the young Finch lacked was *sprezzatura*, an almost untranslatable Italian word whose nearest English equivalent is "unstudied nonchalance," the ability to show a cool lack of concern when the going gets sticky. *Sprezzatura*, according to Castiglione, is the essence of successful courtiership:

> "employ in everything a certain casualness which conceals art and creates the impression that what is done and said is accomplished without effort and even without its being thought about. It is from this, in my opinion, that grace largely derives; for everyone appreciates the difficulty of things uncommon yet well performed, for which reason facility in these things creates the greatest admiration; and on the other hand to strain and, as they say, 'to drag by the hair' imparts the greatest awkwardness and causes everything, no matter how important, to be held in low esteem. Therefore that may be called true art which does not appear to be art."

Blow Not Thy Horn—Too Much

A character in *The Lady's Not for Burning*, by English playwright Christopher Fry, remarks, "I apologize for boasting, but once you know my qualities, I can drop back into a quite brilliant humility." But just how much horn blowing is allowed?

There is, of course, no simple answer. According to Castiglione, a little braggadocio has its place. Here, one of the guests at the castle sounds as if he were talking about any leader who is concerned that his or her contribution to the organization is going unrecognized:

> "But I," Lord Gaspar then replied, "have known few men excellent in anything whatsoever who do not praise themselves; and I think that we can very well bear with them; for when a person who knows he has merit sees that he does not achieve recognition among the unlearned through his deeds, he is resentful that his worth should lie buried and needs must bring it to light in one way or another, in order not to be cheated of the honor which is the true reward of valiant endeavors. . . ."

> Then the Count said:

> "If you had grasped my meaning, I condemned praising oneself shamelessly and inconsiderately, and certainly, as you say, we ought not form a bad opinion of a valorous man who praises himself modestly; however, I take that testimony as more reliable which comes from someone else's lips.

> "Men of outstanding merit should indeed be pardoned when they cherish a very high opinion of themselves; because a man who has great things to do must possess boldness to do them and confidence in himself and not be of abject or cowardly mind, yet be decidedly temperate in speech, seeming not to have so high

an opinion of himself as he actually has, lest that high
opinion pass over into rashness."

A Little Humility Goes a Long Way

It was T. S. Eliot, the poet and critic, who said, "Humility is the
most difficult of all virtues to achieve; nothing dies harder than
the desire to think well of oneself." True enough, but successful courtiers—and leaders—appreciate the fact that a little
humility works wonders. Image inflating, it turns out, usually
doesn't. President John F. Kennedy provided a notable demon-
stration of the power of humility. When he and his wife visited
Paris in 1962, Jacqueline won everyone over—including the
aloof Charles de Gaulle—with her remarkable charm. At the
end of the visit, a press conference was held. Kennedy began it
with these words: "I do not think it is altogether inappropriate
to introduce myself to this audience. I am the man who accompanied Jacqueline Kennedy to Paris, and I have enjoyed it."
Castiglione would have loved this, for he knew that recipients
of great honor should use restraint in accepting it:

> "A man ought always to be a little more humble than his
> rank would require; not accepting too readily the favors
> and honors that are offered him, but modestly refusing
> them while showing that he esteems them highly, yet in
> such a way as to give the donor cause to press them
> upon him more urgently. For the greater the resistance

shown in accepting them in this way, the more will the prince who is granting them think himself to be esteemed."

Pick Your Mentor Well

Nothing can be more important to a career than the help of a mentor. But it is also true that nothing can destroy a career more quickly than choosing an inept mentor. John Dean, one-time counsel to Richard Nixon, had a promising career until Attorney General John Mitchell became his mentor. Both Dean's and Mitchell's careers were destroyed when the Watergate scandal rocked the White House. Castiglione suggests that many successful careers—Alexander the Great's career is one example—have been hugely helped by the choice of the right mentor:

"Although it is almost proverbial that grace cannot be acquired by learning, the man who must learn to be graceful in bodily exercises, assuming first of all that he is not incapable by nature, should begin early and learn the fundamentals from the best masters. How important Philip, King of Macedonia, considered this matter one can understand from the fact that he wished Aristotle, so renowned a philosopher and possibly the greatest that the world has ever known, to be the one who taught the fundamentals to Alexander, his son."

Making the Boss Look Good

An extremely important role in courtiership is helping the prince succeed. This is the courtier's raison d'être. His purpose is not merely to entertain and delight his boss but also to provide—just as a mentor does—wise, and sometimes uncomfortable, counsel:

> "The end of the perfect courtier . . . is to win . . . the goodwill and mind of the prince whom he serves, to such a point that this courtier, without fear or danger of displeasing the prince, can tell and always does tell him the truth concerning everything proper for him to know. And if the courtier knows that the prince's mind is bent on doing something unbecoming, he may dare to oppose the prince and in a courteous way take advantage of the favor acquired through his good traits to draw the prince away from every evil design and lead him into the path of virtue."

Castiglione wrote *The Book of the Courtier* to improve the manners of sixteenth-century Europe. He accomplished his goal primarily because the book celebrated the birth of an entirely new type of human being, Renaissance man. *The Book of the Courtier* has been described, with good reason, as the single most important contribution to the diffusion of Renaissance values. And just as it served as a manual of survival in a very uncertain political period, so, too, can it fulfill this purpose for business leaders in our time.

EIGHT

MACHIAVELLI

Prince of Power

When he wrote *The Prince* in 1513, Niccolo Machiavelli unwittingly established himself as the enfant terrible of power politics, personifying the evil and corruptness in humankind. Even for those who have never read his classic handbook of statesmanship and politics, the word *Machiavellian* suggests duplicity and deceit, someone who values ends over means, views others as useful only as means to achieving his or her purposes, and is unabashedly manipulative.

But Machiavelli did not set out to legitimize wickedness. He simply described, in graphic and frequently brutal detail, how sixteenth-century rulers applied power—how they managed, manipulated, and led. But it is no wonder that history has treated him with monumental unkindness. After all, he committed the unpardonable sin of giving away the "secrets" of princely power. The sanctimonious reaction of Prussia's King Frederick II, who attempted to have *The Prince* banned, was typical:

> I have always considered Machiavelli's *Prince* as one of the most dangerous works ever to be disseminated in the world. It is a book which falls naturally into the hands of princes and of those with a taste for politics. Since it is very easy for an ambitious young man . . . to be corrupted by maxims which flatter the impetuosity of his passions, any book which can contribute to this must be regarded as absolutely pernicious and contrary to the good of mankind.

Frederick's attempt only heightened interest in history's first manual of realpolitik.

The Prince was the literary result of Machiavelli's turbulent political and military career. As a high state official in Florence, he was deeply involved in both domestic and international affairs. His diplomatic reports demonstrate that he was a master at finding the power fulcrum in even the most delicate political situation. He demonstrated military prowess when he directed land and sea operations against Florence's longtime enemy, Pisa. His continued success seemed assured. But when the Italian republic collapsed, Machiavelli found himself out of work, in prison, and suspected of conspiracy. Thanks largely to the efforts of the Medici, who reasserted control in Florence,

Machiavelli was soon released from prison. Nonetheless, he was banished to the countryside.

A letter to a friend describes the melancholy that Machiavelli felt after being thrust out of the center of political action:

> What my life is, I will tell you. I get up at sunrise and go to a grove of mine which I am having chopped down. I spend a couple of hours there, checking up on the work of the previous day and passing the time with the woodcutters. . . .
>
> At nightfall I return home and enter my study. There on the threshold I remove my dirty, mud-spattered clothes, slip on my regal and courtly robes, and thus fittingly attired, I enter the ancient courts of bygone men where, having received a friendly welcome, I feed on the food that is mine alone and that I was born for. I am not ashamed to speak with them and inquire into the reasons for their actions; and they answer me in a kindly fashion. And so for four hours I feel no annoyance; I forget all troubles; poverty holds no fears, and death loses its terrors. I become entirely one of them.

Machiavelli wrote *The Prince* during this enforced sabbatical. It was to have been his entry ticket back into the hotbed of Italian politics. It did not get him a job, but it did make him famous. He had written history's first manual for leaders, replete with case studies whose main players were the heroes of ancient Greece and Rome and of Renaissance Italy.

The Similarity of Corporations and States

Although Machiavelli was writing about the politics of states, much of what he had to say applies equally to modern corporations. Like states, corporations are highly political—preoccupied with the sources and applications of power. Both corporations and states go to great lengths to maintain order and security. A state may apply force to coerce its citizens to lawfulness; corporations can apply such powerful sanctions as transfers, demotions, and terminations. States defend their boundaries by military force; corporations can rely on the weaponry of unbridled competition—industrial espionage, employee pirating, or predatory pricing. And corporations and states are equally territorial, each tenaciously defending its turf.

The Prince was written to instruct princes on the uses and abuses of power in running kingdoms. It is also a classic guide on acquisitions and mergers, emphasizing not the balance and assimilation practiced by Alexander the Great but the Renaissance theme of the individual controlling, sometimes ruthlessly, the organization.

Machiavelli did not write about how life "ought to be," but rather described how successful leaders *actually* work. He made this clear early in *The Prince*:

> It now remains to consider what the attitude and conduct of a prince toward his subjects and friends should be. And since I know that many people have already written about these matters, I fear that I shall be considered presumptuous in writing about them, too, the

more so because in treating this subject I depart from the rules set down by others. But since it is my intention to write something of use to those who will understand, I deem it best to stick to the practical truth of things rather than to fancies. Many men have imagined republics and principalities that never really existed at all. Yet the way men live is so far removed from the way they ought to live that anyone who abandons what is for what should be pursues his downfall rather than his preservation; for a man who strives after goodness in all his acts is sure to come to ruin, since there are so many men who are not good. Hence it is necessary that a prince who is interested in his survival learn to be other than good, making use of this capacity or refraining from it according to need.

How to Manage Acquisitions when the Cultures Are Similar

Machiavelli made two recommendations regarding the management of acquisitions when the cultures of the acquiring and acquired organizations are similar. First, he urged that the old management team be fired. Second, once that had been accomplished, the operation should be left alone.

> To hold them securely, it is enough to have extinguished the line of princes who ruled them formerly and to maintain preexistent conditions. When there is no

change of customs, men will live quietly, as happened in Burgundy, Brittany, Gascony, and Normandy, which have long been a part of France. Though there is some distinction of language among them, the customs are nevertheless alike, and the people can easily get along with each other. Anyone who conquers such territories and wishes to hold on to them must do two things: the first is to extinguish the ruling family; the second is to alter neither the laws nor the taxes. Thus in a short time they will become one with the conqueror's original possessions.

Machiavelli's first recommendation, to remove the rulers, may well seem harsh, especially in light of the recent trend to make the heads of merging companies co-CEOs. Yet, as Machiavelli could have predicted, "sharing" power between individuals who are each used to ruling can create turmoil and rampant rivalries that destroy, rather than secure, a merger, as was the case with the failed Glaxo Wellcome–SmithKline Beecham merger. Appointing coexecutives, observed *The Economist*, "looks like a case of avoiding hard decisions." Machiavelli understood that such "hard decisions" had to be made in order to consolidate power, and removing the rulers does, in fact, still frequently occur. When Wells Fargo bought First Interstate in 1996, for example, one of the first things the company did was to get rid of a number of First Interstate's top executives.[1]

Acquiring executives need to be fully aware of the fear and trembling that they cause. What horrified sixteenth-century princes—the fear of losing job and power—is precisely what makes most modern corporate takeovers "hostile." Usg Corp., for example, a highly profitable building products company that was the low-cost leader in a number of important markets, responded to the threat of corporate raiders with a $3 billion, highly leveraged recapitalization that "tore up the balance sheet" but saved executive jobs.[2] Some vulnerable firms have even made unattractive acquisitions in order to insulate themselves from potential hostile suitors.

Machiavelli's second recommendation was to maintain pre-existing conditions by changing "neither the laws nor the taxes." After rapidly disposing of the old management team, the acquiring company should move much less rapidly, or not at all, in changing anything else.

Unfortunately, this advice is infrequently followed. For example, when Quaker Oats, a food and drinks group, bought soft-drinks maker Snapple in 1994 for $1.7 billion, it could not keep its "hands off." Employees at Snapple were quickly alienated by Quaker's meddling in the company's more "laid-back" culture, and its attempts to force the distribution of Snapple's products through Quaker's channels. Profits quickly disappeared. Three years after buying the company, Quaker sold Snapple for just $300 million.[3]

How to Manage Acquisitions when the Cultures Are Different

For acquirers of firms with vastly different corporate cultures, Machiavelli offered three alternatives: liquidate the acquired

firm; move the CEO to the new location; or establish a management staff of loyal employees and maintain an arm's-length
relationship, simply transferring profits to the parent company:

> When a state accustomed to live in freedom under its
> own laws is acquired, there are three ways of keeping it:
> the first is to destroy it; the second is to go to live there
> in person; the third is to let it continue to live under its
> own laws, taking tribute from it, and setting up a gov-
> ernment composed of a few men who will keep it
> friendly to you. Such a government, being the creature
> of the prince, will be aware that it cannot survive
> without his friendship and support, and it will do every-
> thing to maintain his authority. A city that is used to
> freedom is more easily controlled by means of its own
> citizens than by any other, provided one chooses not to
> destroy it.

Machiavelli's first alternative, to liquidate a captured firm's
assets, is not a uniquely "Machiavellian" tactic. It is as modern
as leveraged buyouts and junk bonds. With hostile bidders
relying more and more on borrowed money to consolidate
their bids, their operating plans look increasingly like liquidation plans. Takeover king Carl Icahn's 1980 purchase of Phillips
Petroleum, for example, would have resulted in stripping
the firm of most of its assets. And the proposed takeover of
Union Carbide, a $9.5 billion giant, by tiny GAF Corporation
(less than one-tenth the size of its target!) during the same
heady era would have required the liquidation of more than

$4 billion worth of Union Carbide assets—a truly Machiavellian dismemberment.

Machiavelli's second alternative, having the CEO move to the new location, is both simple and wise:

> When one acquires states in a province where the language, the customs, and the laws are different, there are difficulties; here both fortune and great ability are needed to keep them. One of the best and most ready solutions is for the new ruler to reside there. This expedient would make the new possession safer and more lasting, as it did for the Turk in the case of Greece. Despite all other measures taken to hold that state, he would have been unable to keep it unless he had gone there to live. Being on the spot, one may observe disorders as they arise and quell them quickly; not being present, one will learn about them only when they have assumed such proportions that they cannot be quelled. Moreover, the new province is not despoiled by the ruler's officials. The subjects are satisfied that they have ready recourse to the prince. Consequently, they have more reason to love him if they choose to be good, and more reason to fear him if they choose to behave otherwise.

Successful CEOs of today's large corporations realize, as did Machiavelli, the need to foster communication among the different parts of their organizations to facilitate employees' "ready recourse" to management. J. Carter Fox, CEO of Chesapeake

Corp., a paper and forest-products manufacturer, requires division heads to "take turns making presentations to the board about the entire company." J. F. O'Reilly, former CEO of H. J. Heinz Co., worked hard to promote communication and camaraderie among company leaders by throwing weekend house parties that combined volleyball and policy making.[4]

And Jack Welch, CEO of General Electric, is a master at staying "in touch" with employees of the huge corporation he rules. Through unexpected visits to plants and offices, lunches with managers several ranks under him, hundreds of handwritten notes to GE people at all levels of the organization, frequent meetings with customers, annual on-site reviews at each of GE's twelve businesses, and appearances at management training sessions, Welch is able, as Machiavelli suggested, to "observe disorders as they arise and quell them quickly." At the same time, his emphasis on communication among those who work at GE ensures that employees' "ready recourse" to management is not eliminated, no matter how far removed they are from the corporate office.[5]

Send In Management Teams

If getting the CEO to relocate is not possible, Machiavelli suggested a third alternative: sending management teams to the newly acquired division. With characteristic boldness, he recommended an aggressive personnel policy upon their arrival. Managers displaced by the "new arrivals" would have limited power or resources to resist:

The next best solution is to send colonies to one or two places which could serve to shackle that state. It is necessary either to do this or to keep a large force of cavalry and infantry there. Colonies do not cost much. Without expense, or with little, they may be sent out and maintained, and they will harm only those whose fields and houses they appropriate for their own use—a minimal part of the population. Those who are harmed, being dispersed and poor, can cause no trouble. All the rest, on the one hand, will be left unharmed (and hence should remain quiet); and, on the other hand, will be fearful lest by some wrongdoing the same that happened to those who were deprived should happen to them. To conclude, such colonies are not costly, are very loyal, and do little harm; those who are hurt, as already indicated, cannot annoy because they are poor and dispersed.

On the Dangers of Trying to Change

A frequent mistake in mergers is trying to change things too rapidly. Most managers do not fully understand the risk that change entails. As Machiavelli argued:

> The difficulties [princes] encounter in winning their dominions arise in part from the new forms of administration and new methods which they are compelled to introduce in order to establish their state and assure their

security. It must be realized that there is nothing more difficult to plan, more uncertain of success, or more dangerous to manage than the establishment of a new order of government; for he who introduces it makes enemies of all those who derived advantage from the old order and finds but lukewarm defenders among those who stand to gain from the new one.

There Is Greater Security in Being Feared than Loved

Today's managers cringe at the Machiavellian admonition that it is better to be feared than to be loved. But Machiavelli had good reason for this apparent heresy. "In the best of worlds," he said,

> . . . it would be best to be both loved and feared. But since the two rarely come together, anyone compelled to choose will find greater security in being feared than in being loved. For this can be said about the generality of men: that they are ungrateful, fickle, dissembling, anxious to flee danger, and covetous of gain. So long as you promote their advantage, they are all yours, as I said before, and will offer you their blood, their goods, their lives, and their children when the need for these is remote. When the need arises, however, they will turn against you. The prince who bases his security upon their word, lacking other provision, is doomed; for

friendships that are gained by money, not by greatness
and nobility of spirit, may well be earned, but cannot be
kept; and in time of need, they will have fled your purse.
Men are less concerned about offending someone they
have cause to love than someone they have cause to fear.

Announce Bad News Immediately

When management has bad news for the troops, as is often true
after a firm has been acquired, Machiavelli recommended dis-
pensing it all at once:

> One ought to consider all the injuries he will be obliged
> to inflict and then proceed to inflict them all at once so
> as to avoid a frequent repetition of such acts. Thus he
> will be able to create a feeling of security among his sub-
> jects and, by benefiting them, win their approval. Any-
> one who acts otherwise, either through timidity or bad
> judgment, will always have to keep a dagger ready in his
> hand, nor will he ever be able to trust his subjects since,
> because of continually renewed injuries, they will never
> be able to feel safe with him. Injuries must be commit-
> ted all at once so that, being savored less, they will
> arouse less resentment.

Machiavelli's admonition that leaders should consider all of
the injuries that they will be obliged to inflict and then proceed
to dispense them all may seem horribly cruel to this century's

readers of *The Prince*. But the psychological wreckage caused by delaying bad news can be more damaging than the news itself. This is particularly true in takeover situations, in which making employees wait interminably before they learn their fate simply increases their fears and hurts productivity. They worry more about getting a new job than about doing well in the one they have.

Bringing Power Out of the Corporate Closet

Niccolo Machiavelli was the first management thinker to bring the subject of power out of the closet. Even so, "power" still conjures up images of managers who exploit others, who coldly and manipulatively make others dependent on them. Power remains a management taboo, much as it was in the sixteenth century, rarely written about and little discussed. Commented Reuben Mark, CEO of Colgate-Palmolive, when asked about executive power: "I don't like to talk about power. I prefer to think about it as responsibility and authority."[6] This unwillingness to talk about power is all the more surprising since social scientists determined decades ago—as had Machiavelli centuries ago—that the most important trait distinguishing successful from unsuccessful managers is that the successful ones are motivated primarily by their desire to possess power.

It is no surprise that power struggles as Machiavellian as those of sixteenth-century Italy do occur in today's business world. Marilyn Moats Kennedy, who, like Machiavelli, specializes in divulging the arcana of power, writes in her book *Powerbase: How to Build It/How to Keep It* that power is the currency of all office relationships. Power, she contends, facilitates cooperation because people just naturally work more readily for those who have clout.[7] Just as earnestly, they overthrow those who do not.

Consider the unhappy—and hugely publicized—removal of Kenneth Olsen, founder and longtime CEO of Digital Equipment Co., following a power struggle in 1992. At one time, Olsen was one of his industry's "visionaries," but when the business environment changed, Olsen could not. Sure that his VAX machines were what the market needed, even as its preference for desktop computers was becoming obvious, Olsen stated: "We always say that the customers are right, but they are not always right." When DEC executives belatedly realized the market had changed and pushed for the company to change as well, Olsen was unwilling to consider it; he had no time for opinions that differed from his own. Ultimately, he was ousted from power, to be replaced by CEO Robert Palmer.[8]

Like it or not, power affects every employee each business day. Managers who aspire to greater success will benefit from understanding it well. For them, *The Prince* is required reading.

NINE

SHAKESPEARE

Timeless Management Insight

Today's corporate leaders frequently "live out" roles astonishingly similar to those of Shakespeare's tragic and archetypal characters. Some organizations are ruled by aging "King Lears," as unwilling to let go of the reins of power as was their counterpart in Shakespeare's ancient kingdom. Frequent are reports of hapless executives who, driven by blind ambition, corrode and then destroy their organizations as surely as did Macbeth in eleventh-century Scotland. And disloyal employees, like archvillain Iago, manipulate their Othello-like colleagues.

Great Men Versus Great Events

Shakespeare's plays are the product of a quintessential Renaissance mentality, a genius more interested in great men—their conflicts and emotions—than in great events. Shakespeare's human characters are consistently presented with such force, in fact, that interest in them often becomes as important as that created by the plot. Harold C. Goddard, who explores Shakespeare's drama in *The Meaning of Shakespeare*, says: "Shakespeare is like life. There are as many ways of taking him as there are ways of living. One by one, all the philosophies have been discovered in Shakespeare's work. . . . The lover, the student, the teacher, the scholar, the director, the actor—every one of them finds something that the other misses."[1] To this list, we must surely add the manager.

Renaissance Psychologist

Like the Greek playwright Sophocles, William Shakespeare (1564–1616) was more psychologist than philosopher. A keen observer of leadership—successful and tragic—and of power (his plays were set in the power center of his day, the king's court), he sought to uncover the hidden thoughts and often-enigmatic actions of his characters in order to reveal their true natures. For this reason, Shakespeare—better than any other Renaissance writer—enables us to plumb the depths of human behavior. His plays are as timely today as when they were written; his characters are as alive for us as they were for his London audiences.

It was Ben Jonson, his close friend and sometime rival, who prophetically observed that he was "not of an age, but for all time." Shakespeare's plays have, for almost four centuries, provided compelling insight into people's behavior and motives, successes and failures, victories and defeats. In his lifetime, he wrote thirty-seven of them, including towering histories, rollicking comedies, and poignant tragedies. Even a casual member of a theater audience will conclude that Shakespeare is, quite possibly, the best observer of human nature and interpersonal relationships in the English-speaking world. The enduring popularity of his plays and his commanding lead in *Bartlett's Familiar Quotations* both attest to this view. He still holds that lead because his plays allow humankind to see itself in all its greatness and its flaws. The things that motivate Lear, Othello, and Macbeth are with us today; human nature, it seems, has not changed.

Shakespeare was not well educated in the formal sense. According to Ben Jonson, he "hadst small Latin and less Greek." Throughout his life, he was much too busy writing, acting, and managing theatrical companies to become a scholar. In his hometown of Stratford, in fact, he was better known as a businessman and investor than as a playwright. His plays lack evidence of impressive historical accuracy or literary erudition. Yet, from boyhood, Shakespeare was endowed with a remarkable sense of observation; a keen sense for people's habits, feelings, and behavior; and a very special ability to discern and to articulate what differentiates one person from another. His avid reading made up for his lack of schooling. He voraciously consumed the great books of his time: Roman poets (especially Virgil and Ovid), Plutarch, Chaucer, Montaigne, even the farcical Rabelais. As A. L. Rowse, the Shakespeare scholar, noted: "Everything about William Shakespeare was surprisingly normal—except, of course, his genius."[2]

And he was an astute politician. Although it would be irresponsible to suggest that Shakespeare wrote his masterpieces simply to impress his royal patrons, the connections are unmistakable at least in the case of his tragedy *Macbeth*. King James I, Shakespeare's patron and protector, assumed the throne just three years before the play was written. He was Scottish; *Macbeth* is the only Shakespearean play based on Scottish history. James preferred short plays; *Macbeth* is Shakespeare's shortest. James was something of an expert on witchcraft, having written a book on the subject; witchcraft pervades the play. Finally, James was a descendant of one of the most important—and most honorable—characters in the play, Macbeth's partner-at-arms Banquo.

King Lear
Management Succession

For the executive who has spent the better part of his or her career getting and keeping power, giving up even a small portion of that power does not come easily. As retirement approaches, it becomes especially difficult. Many senior managers resist letting go of operations that they have built and directed. They find delegating to newly appointed heirs apparent a difficult, if not impossible, task. They know that they will miss the perquisites of leadership. No wonder that when the time comes, many only *appear* to retire. In actuality, they continue to wield great power and influence.

Henry Ford Sr., having set up no management-succession plan whatever, retained the chairman's title and absolute power at Ford Motor Company until he died in 1947 at age eighty-four. In the process, he drove the company to the brink of insolvency. His grandson Henry Ford II, several years before mandatory retirement, turned the company over to Philip Caldwell in 1979. He wisely vacated Ford's world headquarters in Dearborn, Michigan, making it clear that he would no longer be involved in the day-to-day management of the business. But he could not stay away. Only two years later, he quit his new office at Detroit's Renaissance Center and moved back to Dearborn, close enough to look over Caldwell's shoulder.

Such sticking-around seems to be catching. Maurice Raymond "Hank" Greenberg, the seventy-four-year-old CEO of the giant insurer American International Group for more than thirty years, apparently has no immediate plans to step down. Although the naming of his son, Evan, forty-three, as president and chief operating officer was seen as a sign that he was being groomed for the CEO job, Greenberg waves aside questions about retirement plans. "I feel good. I like what I do, and I haven't had another job offer yet," he responds breezily.[3] The failure of a CEO to realize that it's time to leave can be devastating for both the company and the aging CEO, however. Robert E. Allen's refusal to plan his graceful retirement from the top job at AT&T, compounded by his efforts to deny the position to the successor he himself had chosen, kept AT&T in turmoil until the company's board of directors took charge. When the board brought in C. Michael Armstrong as chairman and CEO, Allen was forced to make a humbling exit three years before he had planned to retire.[4]

Moving on is only half the issue, though; the other half is deciding who moves up. "In the past, there was a huge onus on the CEO to groom his own successor," noted Susan Gretchko of

Deloitte & Touche Consulting. But unlike Roberto Goizueta, former chief executive at Coca-Cola, who had well-laid succession plans in place that resulted in a smooth transition of power following his death, many CEOs have trouble planning their own succession. "It's a little like writing a will. Many CEOs don't want to think about it," commented Dennis C. Carey, vice chairman of executive recruiting firm Spencer Stuart. Yet, a quirk of demographics has made the issue of succession planning more critical than ever: of the 500 companies in the Standard & Poor's index, nearly one of every five is headed by a CEO aged sixty-three or older.[5] Consequently, the succession drama could have a long run.

Picking a successor is rarely easy, and there are no general rules for how this task is to be accomplished. At Whirlpool Corp., the names, titles, and photos of the company's top 500 managers are displayed on the walls of a room known as "the bunker." Executives use the room, in which only management-development discussions are permitted, to track the progress of the company's rising stars. At Corning, Inc., chairman and CEO Roger G. Ackerman meets annually with the board to discuss succession issues and planning; directors are given detailed information before the meeting about top candidates for key jobs within the company. And at some companies, the outside directors are taking the lead in succession planning: at Ralston Purina Co. the board encouraged chairman and CEO William P. Stiritz to come up with plans for who would take over from him by linking stock options to his development of a succession plan.[6]

Even when the firm is family owned, picking a successor is no less complicated. One option is to divide the power among siblings, which can lead to vicious battles for control within the family. After Herbert Haft sued his brother and sister in an attempt to win total control of the Dart Group chain and lost, he refused to speak to his brother for fifteen years.[7] Yet, choosing only one offspring as successor can be equally as destructive to family relationships, as George Berkowitz, founder and chairman of the restaurant chain Legal Seafoods Inc., learned. When he chose one of his two sons who were working for the company as his replacement, the other son "walked out and opened his own restaurant. He was very mad, very angry," said Berkowitz.[8]

Shakespeare understood, perhaps better than anyone else, the problem of succession in a family-owned organization. It is the theme of his tragedy *King Lear*, one of his most readable and gripping dramas. *Lear* is a story of filial ingratitude, one in which a leader's foolish fondness for his children leads him to divide his kingdom among them. In modern terms, it is the story of an aging executive who wants to turn the reins of power over to someone else, and of how he selects his replacement. Like many a successful executive, Lear had been respected and loved by his people. His organization had had a long history of stability. The tragedy began only when Lear claimed that he was ready to retire:

> 'Tis our fast intent
> To shake all cares and business from our age,

Conferring them on younger strengths, while we
Unburdened crawl toward death.

Had he only meant it, he, his successors, and his organization might have survived. But because of his unwillingness to
really retire and his inept management-succession plan, his
kingdom was nearly destroyed. Two management lessons in
particular stand out in *King Lear*: (1) the need to find a competent successor upon retirement and (2) the need to let go of
the reins of power to let the successor *succeed*.

Finding a Competent Successor

Lear failed when he tried to pick a successor from among his
three daughters. He planned to decentralize his enterprise by
dividing it into three parts—one for each daughter—and
announced his intention:

We shall express our . . . purpose.
Give me the map there. Know that we have divided
In three our kingdom.

Still, he wanted to screen his candidates one more time. But
having announced his succession plan publicly, he triggered the
very strife that he had hoped to prevent. His selection criterion
was not competence, experience, or even "fit" with the organization's needs; he simply wanted to be flattered:

We have this hour a constant will to [announce publicly]
Our daughters' several [dowries], that future strife

May be prevented now. . . .
Tell me, my daughters
(Since now we will divest us, both of rule,
Interest of territory, cares of state),
Which of you shall we say doth love us most,
That we our largest bounty may extend.

Each candidate who flattered Lear by professing to "love him most" would gain control of a share of the enterprise. First, Goneril:

Sir, I love you more than words can wield the matter;
Dearer than eyesight, space, and liberty;
Beyond what can be valued, rich or rare;
No less than life, with grace, health, beauty, honor;
As much as child e'er lov'd, or father found;
A love that makes breath poor, and speech unable;
Beyond all manner of so much I love you.

Then Regan:

I am made
Of the self-same metal that my sister is,
And prize me at her worth. In my true heart
I find she [exactly describes my love];
Only she comes too short, [in that] I profess
Myself an enemy to all other joys
Which [my senses possess]
And find I am alone [made happy]
In your dear highness' love.

Since both Goneril and Regan met Lear's test, he gave each a third of his kingdom. Finally, he asked his youngest—and favorite—daughter, Cordelia, to respond. She was unwilling to flatter the old king:

Good my lord,
You have begot me, bred me, lov'd me: I
[Am properly dutiful in return],
Obey you, love you, and most honor you.
Why have my sisters husbands, if they say
They love you all? [Perhaps], when I shall wed,
That lord whose hand must take my [marriage pledge]
    shall carry
Half my love with him, half my care and duty.
Sure I shall never marry like my sisters,
To love my father all.

Cordelia's honesty got her fired. Because she said that she loved, respected, and honored her father as a daughter should— no more, no less—rather than pandering to him as her sisters did, Lear disowned her:

Let it be so: thy truth, then, be thy [dowry].
For, by the sacred radiance of the sun,
The mysteries of Hecate, and the night;
By all the [influence] of the [stars]
[By the effect of which] we do exist and cease to be;
Here I disclaim all my paternal care,
[Closeness] and [identity] of blood,

And as a stranger to my heart and me
Hold thee [from this time forth] forever.

Lear was not the only executive to lose his objectivity in the search for a successor. Walter Kiechel, former editor of *Fortune* magazine, observed that "even if you could be objective, what are you going to be objective about? In picking your subordinate's successor—or your own, if you have the wherewithal and the pigheadedness to do it—what are you going to look at? Once you get beyond the bromides—a history of successful performance, proven leadership ability, no known criminal record—you quickly find that even the experts disagree on the criteria to be applied."[9]

There is little question that succession decisions are among the most subjective and intuitive a manager will ever make. But when Lear relied only on flattery, he went too far. It is no wonder that his wrongheaded selection of successors ultimately destroyed his enterprise.

John Bitzer has done it differently. President and chief executive of family-owned Abarta Inc., a Pittsburgh company with interests in publishing, bottling, and oil and gas production, Bitzer is making sure that his successor is chosen primarily on merit. He has removed himself from the process of naming his replacement by putting that responsibility entirely in the hands of Abarta's outside directors. The succession policy means that while two of Bitzer's sons and a nephew work for Abarta, none of them is assured he will ever be CEO. The decision about who will run the company will be based on the needs of the business rather than on personal preference, and Bitzer's relieved he will have no influence on that decision. "I feel like somebody has taken a weight off my shoulders," he said.[10]

LETTING GO

Lear claimed that he wanted to retire. But he was unwilling to let go of his power. After turning his kingdom over to his joint successors, Lear implied—none too subtly—that he would never be far from the center of power. He demanded office facilities and insisted on retaining 100 knights whose salaries were to be paid by the realm. He was even unwilling to give up his title of king. Lear's actions were not unlike those of modern CEOs who insist on retaining the accoutrements of power after they leave office:

> I do invest you jointly with my power,
> Preeminence, and all the large effects
> That troop with majesty. Ourself, by monthly course,
> With reservation of a hundred knights,
> By you to be sustain'd, shall our abode
> Make with you by due turns. Only we shall retain
> The name, and all th' additions to a king.

This arrangement was as unworkable in Lear's ancient organization as it is in a modern one. Within weeks, Lear and his staff had caused so much turmoil by their presence that his daughter Goneril was forced to tell him:

> As you are old and reverend, you should be wise.
> Here do you keep a hundred knights and squires,

> Men so disordered, so debosh'd and bold,
> That this our court, infected with their manners,
> Shows like a riotous inn. Epicurism and lust
> Make it more like a tavern or a brothel
> Than a grac'd palace.

Obviously, Lear did not *really* retire. Like Henry Ford II when he returned to Dearborn, Lear stayed so close to the day-to-day operations of his enterprise that he challenged and stifled the authority of his successors. When Harold Geneen "retired" as chief executive at International Telephone and Telegraph Corp. in 1978, he did not fade away. He stayed on as chairman and consultant to ITT and, when he grew displeased with his handpicked successor, had enough influence with the ITT board to have his successor ousted.

Staying after they have "left" may be therapeutic for aging executives unwilling to face retirement, but it can be a disaster for those left behind who are trying to hold the reins. New CEOs find it impossible to do their jobs well with someone looking over their shoulders. Their positions are undermined when subordinates see that they are not really running the organization.

Examples of thoroughly easy executive transitions are difficult to find, but Robert R. Daniell's efforts to ensure an orderly succession process at United Technologies Corp. certainly stand out. United Technologies had endured an acrimonious succession struggle when Daniell's predecessor, Harry Gray, refused to leave, and newcomer Daniell promised that the next succession would be different. He developed several internal candidates, "a group of a half-dozen of us who went to every board meeting beginning in 1987," said current CEO George David. Giving the candidates broad exposure to the board enabled the directors to be involved from the beginning in evaluating each candidate's potential.

David was named president of United Technologies in 1992, and from then on, Daniell "never allowed any ambiguity about succession whatsoever," said David. David was named CEO in 1994, and then chairman in 1997 when Daniell retired. "Politics in organizations occur when there is ambiguity and uncertainty," noted David. Neither was something Daniell allowed to happen; when he left United Technologies, there was no question about who was in charge.[11] Had King Lear done what Daniell did, his enterprise might not have been destroyed. Instead, he proved that there is nothing as potentially destructive to an organization as a retired executive who cannot let go.

Things get really sticky when children inherit a business. Nervous parents, getting ready to hand over the reins, have been known to concoct odd organizational arrangements in the hope of preventing discord. One founder's widow, for example, has set up a rotating presidency among her three sons. Three brothers who inherited a food and beverage distributorship also rotate the presidency on an annual basis. "From the standpoint of our egos," says one, "it's the only arrangement that makes sense." A pair of Cleveland brothers took extreme, and slightly wacky, measures. For thirty years, they ran their manufacturing business on alternating weeks.[12]

From a management viewpoint, Shakespeare's *King Lear* is a tragedy because Lear failed to understand two managerial precepts: the need to select competent successors and the need to let go. Like many contemporary managers, he led an enterprise that thrived for many years under his leadership. But also like many contemporary managers, he was unable to manage the end of his career and thus destroyed the enterprise. Leaders should remind themselves of the words that Andrew Carnegie had inscribed on his tombstone: "Here lies a man who knew how to enlist in his service better men than himself."

Othello
Intuition Abandoned

Intuition is not a popular word in the lexicon of management. Relying on intuitive hunch instead of rational objectivity has been managerial heresy since Frederick Taylor invented so-called scientific management at the beginning of the twentieth century. Far better, goes the conventional wisdom, to depend instead on hard-nosed logical analysis. The world of managing, it seems, is overwhelmingly "left-brained." Facts are valued over opinions, hierarchy over informality, structure over spontaneity, and analysis over synthesis. Reduce a complex problem to its constituent parts, exhort the management rationalists: recast it in the form of a quantitative model, apply appropriate analytic and quantitative tools (PERT, critical path, and decision trees come to mind), and wait for a solution to present itself in the form of a computer printout.

There is, however, one small problem. Many of the solutions created by this highly quantitative school of management, known to savants as "rationalistic positivism," have been less than superb. These solutions are at least partly responsible for the relative productivity decline in the United States. They have enabled the Japanese to stage impressive invasions into the U.S.

automobile, steel, television, watch, and camera markets. They
have called into question the effectiveness of the nation's business schools, leading many observers to wonder whether those
schools are part of the problem.

Fortunately, there is an antidote to this epidemic of ratio-
nalism. It is called intuition. Placing more reliance on hunch
than on conscious reasoning, intuition requires neither that
managers part with their personal computers nor that they forget about logic. It does, however, require a renewed faith in
subjective "feel" for situations; a willingness to explore the
unknown, to sense possibilities and implications that are not
readily apparent; and a reliance on an uncomfortable kind of
logical process whose steps are often hidden deep in the
unconscious.

AN OCCUPATIONAL HAZARD:
LOSING FAITH IN INTUITION

Unlike the unshakable reliance that most managers typically
place on "the numbers," belief in intuition is largely a matter of
faith. Shakespeare's tragedy *Othello* is a story about how easy it
is to lose that faith. The hero—for whom the play is named—
failed to rely on his intuitive feel at a critical moment in his
career, and the results were disastrous for him and for his organization. And as is so typical in Renaissance literature, a single
individual possessed the power to bring him down.

Othello, the "Moor of Venice," had been a successful military officer, supremely self-controlled, thoroughly sure of his
power and skill. But he was betrayed by Iago, a junior officer

whom he had passed over for promotion. Iago's outrage is understandable: he possessed practical experience, seniority, and impressive references. Yet, Othello selected for the job a man named Cassio, a mere theoretician who had no field experience.

Iago's revenge for this perceived injustice animates the entire play, and his shrewd manipulation of his boss transforms the once alert, decisive, and successful Othello into a pathologically jealous murderer. The tragedy is that Othello makes Iago's task so easy. Instead of trusting his intuition, he abandons it, allowing Iago to manipulate him at will.

Iago began by suggesting, with great subtlety, that Othello's wife, Desdemona, was unfaithful. (She was not.) While Desdemona had an innocent meeting with Cassio, Iago brought Othello into view of the pair and whispered vague insinuations to his commander. Afterward, Iago frequently asked Othello questions that were designed to make him think that there had been some intimacy between Desdemona and Cassio. Othello asked for "hard" evidence:

> Villain, be sure thou prove my love a whore;
> Be sure of it: give me the ocular proof
> Or, by the worth of mine eternal soul,
> Thou hadst been better have been born a dog
> Than answer my wak'd wrath.

Iago provided "evidence" of Desdemona's infidelity in the form of a handkerchief that he dishonestly claimed he had found in Cassio's possession:

IAGO: Tell me but this:
          Have you not sometimes seen a handkerchief,
          Spotted with strawberries, in your wife's hand?

OTHELLO: I gave her such a one: 'twas my first gift.

IAGO: I know not that; but such a handkerchief—
          I am sure it was your wife's—did I today
          See Cassio wipe his beard with.

OTHELLO: If it be that—

IAGO: If it be that, or any that was hers,
          It speaks against her with the other proofs.

A master of innuendo and intrigue, Iago then urged that
Othello guard against being jealous:

     Beware, my lord, of jealousy;
     It is the green-eyed monster which doth mock
     The meat it feeds on.

At first, Othello continued to trust his intuition:

     Think'st thou I'd make a life of jealousy,
     To follow still the changes of the moon
     With fresh suspicions? No; to be once in doubt
     Is once to be resolved. Exchange me for a goat,
     When I shall turn the business of my soul
     To such [blown up, inflated] surmises,

> Matching thy inference. . . .
> Nor from mine own weak merits will I draw
> The smallest fear or doubt of her revolt;
> For she had eyes and she chose me. No, Iago;
> I'll see before I doubt; when I doubt, prove;
> And on the proof, there is no more but this—
> Away at once with love or jealousy.

But Iago continued unrelentingly, reminding Othello of how Desdemona had disobeyed her father when she married him:

> I speak not yet of proof.
> Look to your wife; observe her well with Cassio. . . .
> She did deceive her father, marrying you,
> And when she seem'd to shake and fear your looks,
> She loved them most.

Othello began to consider Iago's words. Iago's "facts" seemed indisputable, his presentation of them flawless. Othello questioned his intuitive—and correct—belief that his wife was not unfaithful. His suspicions began to feed upon themselves. Wracked with self-doubt, he lost all sense of truth. Finally, he became incapable of distinguishing between appearance and reality. Iago had gained complete control of Othello, and he knew it:

> Trifles light as air
> Are to the jealous confirmations strong
> As proofs of holy writ; this may do something.

The Moor already changes with my poison:
Dangerous conceits are, in their natures, poisons,
Which at the first are scarce found to distaste,
But with a little act upon the blood,
Burn like the mines of sulphur.

THE EXECUTIVE IMPOSTER

Othello made the tragic error of abandoning his intuitive perception of the truth and began to see "facts" through another's eyes. A simple man thrust into great power, he began—when he lost faith in his intuitive powers—to suffer terribly from the belief that he was inadequate. Self-doubt may sometimes reflect a flexibility of mind, but Othello went too far:

Rude am I in my speech
And little bless'd with the soft phrase of peace; . . .
And little of this great world can I speak.

Othello apparently believed that people generally overestimated his abilities and that at any moment the truth about his inadequacies would come out. Like leaders profiled by Pauline Clance in *The Imposter Phenomenon*, the greater Othello's achievements, the more he felt that he was perpetrating a fraud and that ultimate failure was inevitable.[13] His reaction was not unusual. According to Clance, 70 percent of successful individuals believe that they have reached their "level of incompetence." The result of this feeling is to make such managers (Othello included) much more susceptible to manipulation by their colleagues. As Othello was skillfully "stage-managed" by Iago, his ability to lead was destroyed.

Iago: Archetypal Organizational Saboteur

Originally, Iago aimed to humiliate Othello and to gain what he considered his rightful position by replacing Cassio as Othello's lieutenant. But as his schemes progressed, he became more and more involved until there was no retreat for him, or for anyone else. Iago's conduct, and its consequences, provide a powerful object lesson of the possible effects of passing over, but still retaining, key members of the organization. When this occurs, as it does regularly in most organizations, it creates the possibility of an organizational saboteur with both the means and the opportunity to do real harm.

Intuition: The Critical Variable

The kind of intuitive sense that Othello gave up may well be the critical variable that separates the successful leader from the unsuccessful one. Those who "listen" to their intuitive inner voices are far less likely than Othello to be manipulated by their "Iagos."

Intuition also provides an ability to anticipate the future, a characteristic that is often attributed to successful leaders. One study found that eleven of the twelve company presidents who had doubled sales in the previous four years scored abnormally high in precognition, the intuitive ability to "see" what is going to happen next. A group of presidents from companies with more modest records exhibited no such special skill. In a similar study, a test of 2,000 managers, Weston Agor of the University of Texas found that top managers rated significantly higher in intuition than did middle- or low-level managers.

Albert Einstein credited his discovery of the theory of relativity to an intuitive "flash of insight." "The really valuable factor," he said, "is intuition." Henry Thoreau had come to the same conclusion. "Knowledge does not come to us by details," he wrote, "but in flashes of light from heaven." And it was an intuitive sense of the marketplace that gave Charles Revson his legendary ability to pick product winners at Revlon. Paul Cook, as head of Raychem Corporation, claimed that nearly all of his decisions were based on intuition; the only ones he regretted, he said, were those not based on it.[14]

Similarly, Ralph Larsen, chairman and chief executive officer of Johnson & Johnson, has claimed: "Every time I have been burned in decision making, it is because I have gone against my instincts."[15] Intuition's place in the corporate world extends beyond personal anecdotes, however. The training of executives in the art of intuition at such Fortune 500 companies as Tenneco and New Jersey Bell, and the establishment of Intuition Clubs at companies such as 3M and DuPont, has led the *Wall Street Journal* to proclaim: "Intuition is *in.*"[16]

What are the components of this apparent capacity to gamble everything and win? Fred Smith, whose fabled Federal Express changed forever the way America ships packages, once told *Inc.* magazine: "I think it is the ability to assimilate information from a lot of different disciplines all at once—particularly information about change, because from change comes opportunity. So you might be reading something about the cultural history of the United States, and come to some realization about where the country is headed demographically."[17]

Whatever its source, intuition is becoming as important as discounted cash-flow projections in leading a successful enterprise. It plays a major role in decisions about product development at Rubbermaid Corp., which produces more than 400 new products a year and consistently appears on *Fortune*'s list of Most Admired Companies. According to CEO Wolfgang Schmitt, developing that many products requires starting with a "huge quantity of ideas"—2,000 to 4,000 a year—then he and his managers go with their intuition to decide which of those ideas to develop further. "Where people go wrong," said Schmitt, "is by spending way too much time analyzing." It's not that he's advocating that thoughtfulness shouldn't be a part of the process: "For the U.S. to compete really well in the world, we have to put more thought content into our products." But at Rubbermaid, gut feel about where to direct that thoughtfulness is a critical part of the equation.[18] And Genentech Inc. CEO Arthur Levinson, who has scrapped a number of projects that didn't appear to be working, has said, "As a manager, it often comes down to intuition. Is it going to work or not?"[19]

Roy Rowan, who scrutinizes the intuitive process in *The Intuitive Manager*, confirms the view that the old-fashioned hunch is a critically important management tool. Rowan reports that Robert Bernstein, the former chairman of Random

House, believes that intuition is the only thing that can protect an executive from the most dangerous individual of all, the "articulate incompetent."[20]

And it could have worked for Othello. But when faced with his articulate (but *not* incompetent) subordinate, he failed to trust his intuition. Instead, he allowed himself to be manipulated. It's not a unique story. Every organization has its Iagos, those people who effectively control others—frequently their bosses. When their motives are honest, everybody benefits. When they are not, as is so dramatically the case in *Othello*, the executive and the organization both suffer. The operative point is that the executive must rely on feeling as well as fact. Doing this does not come easily to executives, whose thought processes are notoriously rigid, logical, analytic, and sequential.

Discounting the inflated claims of the left-brain, right-brain gurus, however, there are a few things you can do to get in touch with your intuition. First, slow down. Let things circle around a bit up there, rather than rushing headlong into that next decision. Your brain is not a decision assembly line in which only quantity counts. Second, learn to see things differently. A large tree, for example, can become a giant green lollipop. This may sound far-fetched. Yet, when Smith conceived of Federal Express, he was thinking about those bank clearinghouses where millions of checks get processed. Voilà! The airfreight's innovative "hub," which made the whole thing possible, was born. Third, put yourself in the other guy's shoes. Usually this means trying to divine what the competition is going to do. But sometimes the competition is just down the hall.

Macbeth
Blind Ambition

Few leadership texts mention "ambition," that elusive desire to succeed. Yet, it is this strong urge to gain ever-increasing amounts of responsibility, power, and income that marks a successful leader. Despite the doubts of social scientists uncomfortable with the linkage of a "self-interest" motive and leadership, let there be no doubt: it is ambition that impels the individual's greatest efforts. And ambition—often to the point of obsession—is the common thread through most high-performing organizations. When ambition is an institutionalized value, a leader's *idée fixe* shared by the members of the organization, it generates near-invincible power.

At Federal Express, the shared ambition was to develop a totally new way to ship freight and information. When financial backers gave up on Smith (and his "crazy" idea), he and his team were undeterred. Their ambition led them to revolutionize the airfreight business. When everyone told Admiral Hyman Rickover that his nuclear navy was a pipe dream, the institutionalized ambition of his elite "nukes" prevailed, producing ships and submarines that could circumnavigate the world's oceans without refueling. At specialty foods and sausage maker Johnsonville Foods, the ambition of CEO Ralph Stayer was to increase sales and profitability at the Wisconsin family-owned business by empowering its employees. He gave them a direct role in everything from writing the manufacturing budget to determining (and doing the discounted cash-flow analysis for) what new equipment was needed. To help them reach personal goals, whether it was learning karate or going back to school, he set up allowances for personal growth projects and scholarships for education. Skeptics, including employees, wondered what he was really up to; "I had to work my fanny off to get people to want to take power," he said. But as employees realized that they had the right to question, to change, to take control of themselves—and when the company's goals were not the boss's, but their own—the ambition to grow the company became everyone's ambition: sales rose more than 15 percent a year, twice as fast as the payroll, and in the first six years Johnsonville doubled its return on assets.[21]

A PROMISING CAREER GONE AWRY

The list of leaders who have succeeded by transforming their personal ambition into a widely held corporate culture could go on and on. But when ambition is *not* shared, when it is a secret, self-serving monomania, it can destroy leaders and organizations. Shakespeare's *Macbeth* is the story of such an ambition, a tragedy of ambition and of colossal evil. In this play we find, as G. Wilson Knight, a leading Shakespeare scholar, puts it, "not gloom, but blackness: the evil is not relative, but absolute."[22] Macbeth is violent and bloody—replete with such actions as regicide, infanticide, stabbings, beheadings, and bludgeonings. It is animated by self-deception and the enigmatic prophecies of three hideous witches. Its initial setting—a black night in the desolate, fogbound moors of Scotland—establishes the brooding sense of doom that pervades the play.

As thane of Glamis ("thane" was a title given the clan chiefs of eleventh-century Scotland), Macbeth was the very image of a successful young nobleman, a medieval fast-tracker and court favorite. He was brave and courageous, his king's most glorious general. He was a "gentle" man, one for whom conspiracy against his king seemed most unlikely. His almost boyish enthusiasm was readily apparent. Upon learning, for example, that the king had just promoted him, Macbeth could not wait to share the good news. He wrote eagerly to his wife:

> "While I stood rapt in the wonder of it, came missives from the king, who all-hail'd me 'Thane of Cawdor,' by which title, before, these weird sisters saluted me, and referred me to the coming on of time, with 'Hail, king that shalt be!' This have I thought good to deliver thee, my dearest partner of greatness, that thou mightest not lose the dues of rejoicing by being ignorant of what greatness is promised thee."

At first, Macbeth showed little outright ambition for the throne. He would bide his time:

If chance will have me king, why, chance may crown me,
Without my [initiative]. . .
Come what come may,
Time and the hour runs through the roughest day.

Only after he heard the witches' prophecy did Macbeth begin to imagine fame that he had never before thought possible. But caught between swelling ambition and loyalty to his king, he was irresolute about how he might turn these dangerous imaginings into reality:

> We will proceed no further in this business:
> He hath honor'd me of late, and I have [won]
> Golden opinions from all sorts of people,
> Which would be worn now in their newest gloss,
> Not cast aside so soon.

Only when the king named as his successor his son, the prince of Cumberland, and thus barred Macbeth's way to the throne, did Macbeth's ambition begin to take control of him:

> The prince of Cumberland! That is a step
> On which I must fall down, or else o'erleap,
> For in my way it lies.

At the same time, Lady Macbeth had been deeply affected by her husband's letter describing his promotion and the witches' prophecy. She decided to leave nothing to chance. She encouraged her husband to do away with the king, knowing that the most direct way to the throne was regicide. But Macbeth's nature was, she feared,

> too full o' the milk of human kindness
> To catch the nearest way. Thou wouldst be great,
> Art not without ambition, but without
> The [wickedness] should attend it.

Lady Macbeth would have none of her husband's thoughtful hesitation. She goaded him on, for, as Macbeth admitted of himself:

> I have no spur
> To prick the sides of my intent, but only
> Vaulting ambition, which o'erleaps itself
> And falls on the other.

She succeeded, providing Macbeth with the spur he needed to murder the king. When the king visited Macbeth's castle at Inverness, Macbeth sneaked into his bedchamber and stabbed him, making it appear that the king's grooms had committed the murder. The heir apparent fled, fearing for his life, and Macbeth was soon crowned.

He acquired all of the titles that the witches had predicted—thane of Cawdor and king of Scotland. But his success quickly became his undoing, for Macbeth was consumed by guilt and overwhelmed by the knowledge that he had sold his soul to the devil. Full of remorse, envy, and distrust—his mind, as he put it, "full of scorpions"—he suffered terrible dreams. As he experienced gradual disintegration, even his once-loving relationship with his wife began to deteriorate. Finally, when he learned that her growing madness (sleepwalking, her eyes wide open, she muttered, "Out, damned spot! out, I say," while constantly rubbing her hands together to wash off imaginary blood) had resulted in her death, he uttered the unforgettable lines that signal the absolute futility of his existence:

> Life's but a walking shadow, a poor player
> That struts and frets his hour upon the stage,
> And then is heard no more; it is a tale
> Told by an idiot, full of sound and fury,
> Signifying nothing.

Macbeth was finally beheaded by an avenging general, the throne was restored, and Scotland was—temporarily, at least—at peace.

An Uncomfortably Familiar Tragedy

Macbeth is a tale of the moral and psychological effects of obsessive ambition on the life of one man. It is also, according to Harold Goddard, who probes Macbeth's psyche in *The Meaning of Shakespeare*, the story of all leaders who yield to obsessive ambition. "Who at one time or another," asks Professor Goddard, "has not been that man? Who, looking back over his life, cannot perceive some moral catastrophe that he escaped by inches? Or did not escape? Macbeth reveals how close we who thought ourselves safe may be to the precipice."[23]

Macbeth is a story uncomfortably close to home. Ambition lies at the core of leadership, and organizations depend above all else on men and women who are impelled by it. But some, for whom ambition becomes obsessive, plunge over the precipice. Consider former CEO Al Dunlap, legendary corporate demolition expert whose cost-cutting tactics increased profits and earned shareholders—and Dunlap—a lot of money. They also earned him the nickname Chainsaw Al. When Dunlap was brought in as chairman and CEO of Sunbeam to rescue the once-renowned but now seriously lagging appliance maker, investors cheered. Living up to his nickname, Dunlap eliminated plants, halved the workforce, and saved more than $200 million in annual costs. But according to an article in *Fortune*, eighteen months after his arrival at Sunbeam, "Chainsaw Al's" ambition was no longer to be known simply as a cost-cutting expert but as a growth expert. Rather than leave, as he usually did once he turned a company around, he vowed to remain at Sunbeam to oversee its growth. And growth certainly appeared evident in year-end results that showed a dramatic increase in sales as well as profits, the introduction of new products, and discussion of a possible major acquisition.[24]

But just a few months later, things began to fall apart. The announcement of a loss in first-quarter earnings was soon followed by news reports that Dunlap had engaged in "bill and hold" practices—booking sales before the goods were delivered. While this sales tactic and accounting practice was not illegal, it greatly inflated 1997 revenues and profits. When Dunlap's longtime ally, chief financial officer Russell Kersh, then acknowledged to the board that sales for the second quarter were "a little soft," and Dunlap reportedly demanded the board's support or he and Kersh would resign, the directors became concerned enough to start questioning other Sunbeam executives. What they learned, including the fact that the second quarter would be far below Dunlap's forecast and that the company was in serious trouble, led them to ask Dunlap for his resignation. "We lost our confidence in him, and the ability to sustain things was questionable," said Sunbeam director William T. Rutter.[25]

The 1980s "Decade of Greed" story of Dennis B. Levine is another classic case study in the destructiveness of obsessive ambition. At thirty-three, he was the $1-million-a-year managing director of Wall Street's Drexel Burnham Lambert, Inc., and his career, like Macbeth's, was entirely promising. He had what one Wall Street observer called "star quality," the ability to know what was about to happen in the market. But he was also, according to the *New York Times*, a person with an insatiable desire to succeed who worked relentlessly to become rich, powerful, and famous.[26] It was, in fact, his "vaulting ambition" that prompted the head of one merger-and-acquisition department to give him his first job. But Levine's career crashed when the U.S. Securities and Exchange Commission alleged in May 1986 that he had illegally used his position as a top merger specialist to trade in the stocks and options of dozens of companies that he knew were about to be bought, in this way netting more than $12 million in less than five years.

IMBALANCED ANALYSIS AND ACTION

There is another important lesson in *Macbeth*. Besides obsessive ambition, Macbeth had a second flaw: he consistently failed to analyze fully the situations in which he placed himself. He doubted the witches' prophecies, yet he quickly moved to fulfill them. Although an intuitive "inner voice" repeatedly urged him to wait, he listened instead to the reckless counsel of his closest adviser, his wife. He was confronted with frightful visions just before he murdered the king, yet he proceeded. He was a man of too little analysis and too much action. Caught up in the path he had pursued, one born of hasty, ill-considered action, he was led inexorably toward his doom— and he knew it:

> I am in blood
> Stepped in so far that, should I wade no more,
> Returning [would be] as tedious as [going] o'er.
> Strange things I have in head, that will to hand,
> Which must be acted [without being properly studied].

John Connors, who analyzes Macbeth's leadership style in his essay "Analysis, Action, and the Role of the Manager," asserts that good leadership comes from achieving a balance between analysis and action. Leaning too far one way or the other can be disastrous. Macbeth made the error committed by any leader who overemphasizes action at the expense of analysis. Connors believes Macbeth had become obsessively committed to a course of action and therefore, despite the warning signs, plunged ahead single-mindedly and completed his evil task."[27]

DESTRUCTIVE AMBITION

Ambition is a necessary—and usually positive—motivator of leaders. Nothing great happens in organizations without it. This was as true for Macbeth's Scotland as it is for General Motors or IBM. Harvard psychologist David C. McClelland and con-sultant David H. Burnham, whose *Harvard Business Review* article "Power Is the Great Motivator" investigates the role of ambition, have isolated three important leadership motives. There are leaders who are motivated primarily by the need for "affiliation," which—loosely translated—means simply the desire to be liked by others. These teddy bears "make so many ad hominem and ad hoc decisions," according to McClelland and Burnham, "that they almost totally abandon orderly pro-cedures." High-need-for-affiliation leaders stay on good terms with almost everyone (and thereby frequently suffer the dis-tinction of getting very little done). Then there are leaders who are motivated primarily by the need to "achieve." McClelland and Burnham's research showed that such leaders possess a high desire to do challenging and competitive work. These high-achiever dynamos thrive on difficult goals, enjoy risk taking, and are willing to assume full responsibility for solving sticky problems.

McClelland and Burnham discovered that the third motive, power, is the real engine behind effective leadership. Raw power, their study showed, is more important than being liked or feeling like a winner. However, the researchers differentiated between power that is directed toward personal aggrandize-ment (possessed by leaders who show little self-control, are impulsive, drink too much, and tend to collect symbols of per-sonal prestige such as fancy cars and big offices) and power that is beneficial to the organization (the kind possessed by leaders who want to serve others and are more "institution minded").[28]

Macbeth, of course, allowed his need for power to become corrosive and all-consuming. Instead of applying ambition to serve the needs of his organization, Macbeth became obsessed with obtaining greater power and fame. In grasping madly for them, he destroyed himself and wreaked havoc in his organization. The lesson here is that ambition, when shared, is a creative and positive force. But when it is based only on self-interest, it can demolish the organization.

PART THREE

THE INDUSTRIAL AGE

Triumph of the Organization

The Industrial Era, since it is "our" own, is difficult to describe and even more difficult to analyze. Those who study it are too close to it to be able to understand it fully. They lack one of the key requisites for scholarly objectivity: an adequate historical perspective. Nonetheless, their musings, hypotheses, and hunches—however tentative—help provide insight into a relationship between individual and organization that is dramatically different from the relationship between individual and organization that existed during the classical period and the Renaissance. Unlike the ancients, who were preoccupied with achieving balance between the needs of the individual and the needs of the organization, and unlike Renaissance man, whose individual powers regularly eclipsed those of the "establishment," industrial man is overwhelmingly dominated by the organization. This unbalanced relationship is not unprecedented: medieval man, for example, was dominated by a distant but all-powerful organization—the church. But the degree to which modern institutions have come to shape, guide, and not infrequently control individual behavior is unparalleled in the history of humankind. Ralph Waldo Emerson, the nineteenth-century American essayist and philosopher, captured this tendency of economic organizations to dominate when he wrote: "Things are in the saddle and ride mankind."

The classics profiled in this section can help leaders to cope better as members in a society dominated by large organizations.

In this part, we probe the views of some writers who have lived in and observed the Industrial Era. In his essay "Reflections on the Revolution in France," Edmund Burke challenges the *sine qua non* of modern organizations, innovation-at-any-cost, and makes an urgent plea for the development of a sense of history. The principle that survival depends primarily on the ability to adapt, advanced by Charles Darwin in *The Origin of Species*, is one that may be applied—with some caveats—to the rise and fall of modern organizations. John Stuart Mill's essay "On Liberty," the most articulate statement ever made on the importance of tolerating disagreement, provides a persuasive argument for democratic management and individual freedom in modern organizations. Henry Thoreau's "Walden," in which the author contends that small is better, brings into dramatic relief some of the reasons why "merger mania" so infrequently enhances value to stockholders. Arthur Miller's play *Death of a Salesman* provides unmistakable evidence of the damage that can be done when, for whatever reason, a person finds himself or herself in the wrong job. Finally, Ernest Hemingway's novel *For Whom the Bell Tolls* is an unforgettable tale of the turnaround manager—that special breed of leader who, before he does anything else, must win the loyalty of demoralized and suspicious employees.

The Birth of the Corporation

With its roots in the rapid economic development of eighteenth- and nineteenth-century Europe, the Industrial Era brought with it much more than just machines and the factory system. It brought an entirely new way of life. Tens of thousands of farmers left the countryside to work in urban factories. And with mechanization, the era of the small, one-owner factory came to an end, since the capital required for complex machinery outgrew the capacity of all but a few individual entrepreneurs.

Thus was born the keystone of the Industrial Era, the modern corporation. It was an institution that would forever change the relationship between the individual and the organization. The corporation made it possible for legal ownership to become separated from the day-to-day work of running the business. Work relationships once based largely on intimate personal contact were replaced by a system in which individuals were interchangeable, much like parts in a machine. Individuals became less significant—even in their own eyes—as they confronted this vast organization that was beyond their control and often beyond their comprehension. The corporation required new levels of specialization of labor, central coordination, economies of scale, and concentrated decision making.

It precipitated a rush from individualism to collectivism. Renaissance tendencies toward individual honor, glory, and entrepreneurship were replaced, with few exceptions, by the collective management of "organization man" and the pursuit of the modern era's overarching goal, "maximum efficiency." As the organization grew bigger, the individual grew smaller. Erich Fromm, who pondered industrial man's mental health in *The Sane Society*, wrote of a new kind of determinism. "The manager, like the worker, like everybody, deals with impersonal giants: with the giant competitive enterprise; with the giant national and world market; with the giant consumer, who has to be coaxed and manipulated; with the giant unions, and the giant government. All these giants have their own lives, as it were. They determine the activity of the manager and they direct the activity of the worker and clerk."[1]

Industrial man changed in other ways as well. According to David Riesman, who analyzed modern social and character structure in *The Lonely Crowd*, a shift in values occurred, a shift from "inner-direction" to "other-direction."[2] Riesman argued that Renaissance man, with his highly individualized character, possessed a kind of "internal gyroscope" that kept him on course even in the midst of pressures to conform. He was "inner-directed." Industrial man, however, depending less on himself than on others for direction and approval, replaced the gyroscope with a kind of wide-ranging "radar set" to receive myriad signals from others, including his contemporaries, the mass media, and—perhaps most important—his workplace in the modern corporation. Riesman believed that the Industrial Era's advances in science, technology, and efficiency came at a very high cost—individual autonomy.

It is this subordination of selfhood to external authority that led John Kenneth Galbraith, longtime critic of the corporate world, to observe: "Unlike the old capitalist or the self-made man, the modern executive surrenders his body and, so far as available, his soul to the organization, and it is the terms of this surrender that remain to be explored, along lines already laid down by Joseph Heller in *Something Happened*. The pay, stock options, golden parachutes, retirement benefits, and other perquisites, not excluding the company jet, are fine. But their price is the subordination to the purpose of the organization of all public and most private speech, a self-censorship that is made tolerable only by being habitual and unrecognized."[3]

The Birth of the Bureaucracy

Ironically, in a society founded on individual self-sufficiency and the Jeffersonian sentiment that the best government is that which governs least, bureaucracy is fast becoming the prevailing organizational form. Its essence is administrative hierarchies, standardized working procedures, elaborate timetables, rigid policies, central control, and—perhaps most insidious—an inexorable tendency to grow. Large organizations are usually administered through mazes of departments and subdivisions managed by officials who, for the most part, follow impersonal and inflexible routines. A look at the number of levels of management in modern corporations provides stark evidence of a teeming bureaucracy in action. Many corporations have at least eight levels of management, and some have eleven or twelve. The consequence is managers with a very narrow span of control and only a fraction of a job to perform.

It is the rapidly expanding bureaucracy that has contributed most to a loss of autonomy. There is, however, another kind of alienation, one that Karl Marx, the nineteenth-century German philosopher of history, envisioned and wrote about in his little-known and even less read *Economic and Philosophical Manuscripts*. This alienation, an outgrowth of large-scale production and the bureaucratization that so frequently accompanies it, occurs when workers feel that they do not have an active and important role in the production process. Marx believed that the special skills of each individual—which once provided the important psychic rewards of autonomy and self-expression—had become insignificant in the maws of giant, and capitalist-owned, organizations. Work, he thought, would become not an end unto itself, but merely a means to an end, no longer capable of providing the worker with any benefit save subsistence.

Conformity Versus Individualism

As organizations overwhelm the individual, conformity becomes one of society's most cherished values. From corporate dress codes to subtly imposed political views, agreement and consensus have become standard features of the Industrial Era. Increasingly, "organization men" succeed. Iconoclasts do not. Challenging the conventional wisdom may be acceptable deportment for poets, dreamers, and an occasional entrepreneur, but it is behavior that, while given lip service, is rarely countenanced, and frequently penalized, in large organizations. The unwillingness to countenance disagreement has adversely affected the quality of decision making, since consideration of alternatives—especially those that are at odds with the conventional wisdom—is a very necessary part of good decision making. So critical is this problem that some experts have recommended nothing less than a revival of one of humankind's oldest forms of organized dissent, the "devil's advocate."[4] This person would occupy a newly created office of official "naysayer" and be charged with the responsibility of pointing out flaws in proposals. The idea that disagreement and constructive debate be institutionalized provides convincing evidence of the Industrial Era's pervasive drive for conformity.

TEN

EDMUND BURKE

Look Backward Before Leaping Forward

When Henry Ford told a *Chicago Tribune* reporter in 1916 that "history is more or less bunk," he expressed a near-universal and long-enduring human sentiment. Ford unwittingly echoed the eighteenth-century French writer Voltaire, who more than a hundred years before Ford had testily dismissed history as nothing more than "a pack of tricks we play on the dead." And 2,000 years before that, Polybius—ironically one of the most famous of ancient historians—contended that history could not compete with the present for human interest. "In all the vast variety of disorder, struggles, and changes . . . [introduced] into human life," he said, "we shall find none equal to . . . none worthy to be compared for their importance with those events that have happened in the present age." Disdain for history, it seems, has long been a very common frame of mind.

For most people—especially businesspeople—a kind of single-minded fascination with future progress and possibility has made looking carefully at the past, and even at the present, seem to be a useless preoccupation. Americans in particular have long cherished the dream of what "might be" more than the reality of what "has been" or "what is." This is not surprising. The notion of "progress"—of inexorable change from lower to higher states of knowledge and well-being—has been a vital part of the psyche of the Western world since the time of the Greeks. It is so powerful a thread in the West's cultural fabric that Robert Nisbet, who examined its role in *History of the Idea of Progress*, concluded that "if the idea of progress does die in the West, so will a great deal else that we have long cherished in this civilization."[1]

Exploding the Japanese Management Myth

But balancing our overwhelming futurism with a modicum of historical perspective can be hugely, and often surprisingly, informative—particularly in business. It can separate myth from reality. Consider the widely held belief that the recent industrial success of Japanese firms is due primarily to cultural differences between East and West. These differences are said to manifest themselves in such "Japanese" managerial customs as lifetime employment, seniority-based compensation, and a paternalistic management philosophy. Thus, many observers express amazement when a U.S. company is able to "import" Japanese management styles. But it turns out that the "cultural characteristics" argument does not stand up under the test of historical investigation, as Barbara S. Lawrence reports in her *Academy of Management Review* article "Historical Perspective: Using the Past to Study the Present." Lawrence reports on a study of the personnel records of the Kikkoman Shoyu Company since 1918. The study found that, over a sixty-year period, considerable variation existed in the actual practice of lifetime employment, seniority-based compensation, and family-firm ideology. It was, in fact, *not* cultural differences but economics—the effects of World War II and the "Westernization" of Japan's industrial community—that had the greatest impact on the presumably traditional Japanese employment practices. Lawrence found that these practices were highly transitory and not, as many had believed, a permanent industrial fixture deeply rooted in the Japanese society. Historical perspective enabled her to see through the mist of popular mythology to the facts.[2]

The "Father of Conservatism"

No one has ever argued more effectively that leaders need a keen sense of historical perspective than Edmund Burke, the eighteenth-century British statesman, parliamentary orator, and political thinker. A tall and ungainly Irishman, Burke played a prominent role on England's political scene from 1765 until his death in 1797, and he remains today an influential figure in the history of political theory. Blessed with tremendous

self-confidence, he is best known for a speech he made to his
Bristol constituency in 1774, in which he told his listeners that
he would follow the dictates of his own knowledge rather than
their desires. "Your representative," he said, "owes you, not his
industry only, but his judgment; and he betrays instead of serving you if he sacrifices it to your opinion." These strong words
placed Burke in direct opposition to many of his constituents,
and cost him his seat in parliament in the next election.

When the French Revolution broke out in 1789, most
Englishmen greeted it with great enthusiasm. But Burke was
shocked by its disregard for history and tradition and alarmed
at the favorable reaction of his countrymen. He considered the
revolution to be an unmitigated evil. Concerned that the revolt
of the "uncontrollable masses" might spread into England, he
wrote an essay so sweeping in scope that his contemporary Sir
Gilbert Elliot insisted that it "contains the fundamental elements of all political knowledge." It was to become the bible of
modern conservatism. In "Reflections on the Revolution in
France," Burke criticized the French Revolution as an unprecedented and dangerous innovation and developed a counterthe-
ory of reform that tolerated reform of society's ancient order
but not its destruction. Since this work defended tradition, rev-
erence for history, and the hereditary right of kings and the
aristocracy, it is no surprise that George III was one of its greatest promoters. Burke's essay was, the king said, "a good book,
a very good book, and every gentleman ought to read it."

"Reflections on the Revolution in France" is a wide-ranging
literary masterpiece, covering subjects as disparate as the value

of tradition, the importance of an individual's membership in a group, and the effective management of change. In it, Burke reviewed the actual course of the French Revolution and examined the motives and personalities of the people who led it. He tried to uncover the basic ideas that animated the rebellion against the French monarchy. Mostly, though, he attacked the revolution for its essential denial of tradition and its disrespect for history. And, lest the British make the same mistake, he contrasted it with England's long-standing respect for traditional wisdom and broad historical perspective.

What we did today, said Burke, should be a continuation of what we did yesterday. A complete break with the past was unthinkable. For example, Burke saw the Declaration of Right, written in 1689 during the reign of William and Mary, connected with and emerging from the Magna Carta of 1215:

> From Magna Carta to the Declaration of Right, it has been the uniform policy of our constitution to claim and assert our liberties, as an entailed inheritance derived to us from our forefathers, and to be transmitted to our posterity; as an estate specialty belonging to the people of this kingdom, without any reference whatever to any other more general or prior right. By this means our constitution preserves a unity in so great a diversity of its parts. We have an inheritable crown; an inheritable peerage; and House of Commons and a people inheriting privileges, franchises, and liberties, from a long line of ancestors.

History as Organizational Stabilizer

People in corporate organizations, like those in states, need to have a sense of their relationship not only with the organization's present and future, but with its past as well. This is particularly important in times of change. Rosabeth Moss Kanter, in *The Change Masters*, observes that it is during times of change that people find stability and security in the culture and long-term direction of the organization. "It requires," she says, "that they feel integrated with the whole rather than identified with the particular territory of the moment, since that is changeable."[3] Leaders can reduce the trauma of a change by demonstrating that the change is not discontinuous, that it is a natural outgrowth of the organization's "inheritance" from the past.

A sense of the organization's past is also critical in knowing the direction that change should take within an organization. A look at reasons for corporate failure points to the fact that senior executives often don't know their company's history, don't understand the company's "core expertise." Noted Stephen Fraidin, a partner at the Wall Street law firm of Fried Frank Harris Shriver & Jacobson: "It is a stunning if disturbing fact of corporate life in the 1990s: A lot of senior people at very large companies have no idea what made their organization successful."[4] Without an understanding of the factors that helped build a successful enterprise, executives may advocate change that destroys the very essence of the company's success.

It's a lesson that office furniture giant Steelcase, a nearly ninety-year-old, privately owned company, learned the hard way. The company had a legacy of trust and teamwork that evolved under management "that saw the business beyond its commerce potential, as a social entity that could help people achieve their dreams," said CEO James Hackett, a fourteen-year veteran of Steelcase when he was picked to lead the company in 1995. In the early 1990s, however, management was more focused on profits than people, he said, an error in judgment that ultimately hampered growth. Failing to understand how employees' pride in working together to achieve results contributed to the company's success, management made decisions based only on the bottom line. Jobs were eliminated, trust in management eroded, morale slumped, profits plunged, and discontented workers threatened to unionize.

Hackett, perhaps unwittingly, applied Burke's philosophy in his efforts to revitalize the company. He understood the need for Steelcase—with 23 percent of the market, double that of each of its main competitors—to change, not only to keep its lead in the marketplace but also in order to anticipate and design workspaces for the future. But he also understood that change at the expense of the core values that are the company's link with the past—its dedication to developing people, and to making them feel an integral part of the company—would fail. His strategy to help the company's 20,000 employees again feel a part of "a warm, fuzzy, small, family business" included a weekly E-mail letter to all of them which covered everything from his plans for the company to how he conquered his dislike of giving speeches. Morale returned, profits increased, and employees—again feeling that they were part of the team— embraced ideas for making Steelcase stronger and more innovative.[5]

Hackett's strategy for change at Steelcase corresponds with Burke's argument that stability and a sense of "changelessness" seem to be necessary ingredients for change. Just as Burke fostered the stability of his nation by associating seventeenth-century England with thirteenth-century England, a corporate culture provides stability by linking the organization with its heritage. It is a paradox that the organizations that are most likely to be able to change with the times are those that have the most internal stability.

Innovation Versus Reform

On the subject of innovation, Burke offers a refreshing, and a bit shocking, perspective that is rarely seen in twentieth-century management literature:

A spirit of innovation is generally the result of a selfish temper and confined views. People will not look forward to posterity who never look backward to their ancestors. . . . Our political system is placed in a just correspondence and symmetry with the order of the world, and with the mode of existence decreed to a permanent body composed of transitory parts, wherein, by the disposition of a stupendous wisdom, molding together the great mysterious incorporation of the human race, the whole, at one time, is never old, or middle-aged, or young, but, in a condition of unchangeable constancy, moves on through the varied tenor or perpetual decay, fall, renovation, and progression. Thus, by

preserving the method of nature in the conduct of the
state, in what we improve, we are never wholly new; in
what we retain, we are never wholly obsolete.

Burke did not deny that change was sometimes necessary.
He had, in one of his first publications, the *Abridgement of
English History*, acknowledged as much after his study of the fall
of Rome. "We are," he said, "in a manner compelled to
acknowledge the hand of God in those immense revolutions, by
which, at certain periods, he so signally asserts his supreme
dominion, and brings about that great system of change, which
is, perhaps, as necessary to the moral as it is found to be in the
natural world." But he did take great pains to differentiate innovation from reform. To Burke, "innovation" derived from the
confined view that newness is good for its own sake. He always
used the term to mean revolutionary or radical change.
"Reform," on the other hand, was temperate, slow, and reasoned. It allowed for growth and further development. Reform
accomplished changes, however important they might be, cau-
tiously and gradually. Unlike innovation, reform constituted
sound and healthy social change. Burke's notion of reform was
that it must always relate change to the conservation and bet-
terment of the existing structure.

Burkean Philosophy at the Pentagon

Some contemporary managers may see Burke's point of view as
agonizingly slow incrementalism. More in favor of the "big
bang" theory of change, these managers strive to make the one

change, or simultaneous group of changes, that will move the company in one leap to the desired end result. Research on why organizational change fails, however, has shown that such radical change seldom works. Further, in what could be a contemporary rewrite of Burke's viewpoint, the research indicated that "successful change is more often the result of a series of carefully thought-out actions designed to move a company in the desired direction."[6]

A survey by *Fortune* magazine on why companies fail offers further verification of Burke's belief in the importance of cautious and gradual change. The consensus of a wide variety of management experts was that the propensity of some executives to move from one management fad to the next—apparently looking for the "big bang" that worked—created for their organizations a workforce increasingly resistant to change. These employees, suffering from what Peter Scott-Morgan, a director at giant consulting firm Arthur D. Little, called "change fatigue," begin to reject any new initiatives, further frustrating management and leading to even more radical moves to try and effect change. The strategy doesn't work. Noted Scott-Morgan, clearly a proponent of careful and reasoned change, "There is no evidence anywhere that ramming something down people's throats is an effective management tool."[7] Another proponent of incremental change is General John Vessey, former chairman of the U.S. Joint Chiefs of Staff. Under considerable pressure in 1984 to change the role of the Joint Chiefs, Vessey cautioned against radical change. "There are two ways to make things get better," he said in a *Wall Street Journal* interview. "One way is to whittle away at what can be changed. The second is to have radical reorganization. My view is that the first is probably better, if you can do it that way."[8] Burke would have agreed wholeheartedly.

For managers (or management consultants) thinking about embarking on efforts to foment "revolutionary" rather than "evolutionary" change in their organizations, Burke had some sobering thoughts:

> The errors and defects of old establishments are visible and palpable. It calls for little ability to point them out; and where absolute power is given, it requires but a word wholly to abolish the vice and the establishment together. . . . To make everything the reverse . . . is quite as easy as to destroy. No difficulties occur in what has never been tried. Criticism is almost baffled in discovering the defects of what has not existed; and eager enthusiasm and cheating hope have all the wide field of imagination, in which they may expatiate with little or no opposition.
>
> At once to preserve and to reform is quite another thing. When the useful parts of an old establishment are kept, and what is superadded is to be fitted to what is retained, a vigorous mind, steady, persevering attention, various power of comparison and combination, and the resources of an understanding fruitful in expedients, are to be exercised. . . . But you may object—"A process of this kind is slow. It is not fit for an assembly, which glories in performing in a few months the work of ages. Such a mode of reforming, possibly, might take

up many years." Without question it might; and it
ought. It is one of the excellencies of a method in which
time is amongst the assistants, that its operation is slow,
and in some cases almost imperceptible.

To Preserve and Reform

Burke believed that the "traditions" of an organization (today
we would call them its "corporate culture") have great value.
They are the storehouse of the organization's collective wisdom.
These traditions grow out of the past and are adapted to the
present without any break in continuity. A manager who does
not recognize their importance can easily destroy, but not easily rebuild, them. Any effort to change the organization, therefore, should be implemented slowly, a little at a time; and always
carefully, so that the changes are in agreement with its history
and its tradition. Great managers, Burke suggests, avoid the
extremes of destroying the existing order or of resisting change
at all costs. He argues for a style of managing that preserves and
reforms, that strikes a balance between preservation and
change. John Gardner, author of *Self-Renewal,* agrees. "Mes-
merized as we are by the very idea of change," he says, "we must
guard against the notion that continuity is a negligible—if
not reprehensible—factor in human history. It is a vitally
important ingredient in the life of individuals, organizations,
and societies."[9]

  In support of that idea, Richard Neustadt and Ernest May,
both of whom teach at Harvard's John F. Kennedy School of
Government, have for a number of years taught a course that

demonstrates how history has been used—and abused—by leaders. When asked why anybody in business would be interested in history, May replied: "Mainly because it can reduce the number of mistakes you make. We have developed a series of questions to ask yourself before taking action. They'll help you learn how to think historically. Good decision makers almost instinctively put a problem into a historical context. You can be successful up to a point with a quick-fix approach, but thinking historically is the mark of effective leadership and decision making."[10]

Some firms, aware of gaping holes in their company's history, have hired professional historians to remedy the problem. Wells Fargo Bank in San Francisco, for example, has established a history department staffed by thirteen professionals. Its purpose? To provide historical perspective for a staff wracked by high turnover and frequent transfers. Texaco, Boeing, Eli Lilly, Eastman Kodak, and GE also have history staffs. To no surprise, it is firms that are undergoing rapid change that are most interested in providing a sense of the organization's history to their employees.

The lesson of all this is that understanding an organization's history may be as important as understanding what you want its future to be. There are few genuinely "breakthrough" organizational transformations. More typically, what appear to be revolutionary changes turn out to be—when carefully analyzed—merely the sum total of small past adjustments, a kind of "logical incrementalism" that links the future of the organization inexorably to its past.

Edmund Burke defined a new and critical role for the effective manager—that of part-time historian. The manager who is unaware of his or her organization's history cannot fully understand the dynamics of projects that are already under way or are envisioned for the future. Again, Rosabeth Moss Kanter:

> In conceiving of a different future, change masters have to be historians as well. When innovators begin to define a project by reviewing the issues . . . they are not only seeing what is possible, they may be learning more about the past; and one of the prime uses of the past is in the construction of a story that makes the future seem to grow naturally out of it in terms compatible with the organization's culture. The architecture of change thus requires an awareness of foundations—the bases in 'prehistory,' perhaps below the surface, that make continued construction possible.[11]

Debunking Henry Ford

The manager's job has always been a multifaceted one. To add part-time historian to the job description may seem overly demanding. But in times of rapid change, a sense of organizational continuity based on historical perspective may be as necessary as an awareness of where the business's markets are headed. History, it turns out, is *not* bunk, as an older but wiser Henry Ford evidently discovered late in his career. He ordered the following words to be emblazoned over the entrance to the Ford Museum in Dearborn, Michigan: "The farther you look back, the farther you can see ahead." These are wise words for business leaders in the midst of unprecedented change.

ELEVEN

JOHN STUART MILL

Participative Leadership

In his encyclopedic study of more than 3,000 books and articles on leadership, Ralph Stogdill concludes that "four decades of research on leadership have produced a bewildering mass of findings. Numerous surveys of special problems have been published, but they seldom include all the studies available on a topic. It is difficult to know what, if anything, has been convincingly demonstrated by replicated research. The endless accumulation of empirical data has not produced an integrated understanding of leadership."[1]

Confused Leaders

Where does this leave practicing leaders? Probably more confused than ever, if they rely on the baffling plethora of leadership theory. There are "trait" theories, "behavioral" theories, and "contingency" theories. There are the "managerial grid" and "system 4." There are "boss-centered" leadership and "subordinate-centered" leadership—"autocratic" and "laissez-faire" leadership. The manager can choose between "country club" and "middle of the road" management styles. There are the Theory X leadership style, the Theory Y leadership style (discussed earlier), and even a Theory Z leadership style. Something for everyone, but nothing that sufficiently answers the question "How do effective leaders lead?"

Democratic Leadership at W. L. Gore

One thing *is* clear, though. Leadership styles vary by organization. And organizations range from those that are highly participatory to those that are near-dictatorships. At W. L. Gore and Associates, for example, the emphasis is on participative leadership. No company gives its employees more opportunity to participate in decisions than does this producer and marketer of Goretex, a space-age fabric.

The organization structure of the firm is the antithesis of the traditional pyramidal hierarchy. In an adaptation of and improvement on the "matrix" organization form, the company has invented what the late Bill Gore called a "lattice" organization. In it, every "associate" (there are no "employees") is encouraged to work with every other associate in a kind of corporate free-for-all that would overwhelm even the trendiest management consultant. The firm violates almost all of the traditional management principles. There is no chain of command, no hierarchy. People have no titles. The boss doesn't give orders; in fact, there are no bosses, only "sponsors." There is no fixed or assigned authority. And no fixed assignments—multidiscipline teams organize themselves around projects as they emerge. When new associates are hired, they are told to look around and find something they'd like to do. Like the Greek philosopher Plato, Gore limited the size of his utopia: 200 people per plant. Result? Gore Associates has forty-five technology and manufacturing sites in the United States, Europe, and Asia-Pacific. Profits are shared with the associates, and there is a stock ownership plan.[2]

"In a strange way," said *Forbes* magazine, "through intensely profit motivated capitalism, the Gores have realized an old Marxist ideal, eliminating the alienation between work and worker and giving the worker the fruit of his labor." Appropriately enough, the management style at Gore is called "un-management." Founder Bill Gore put it plainly: "We can't run the business. We learned over twenty-five years ago to let the business run itself. Commitment, not authority, produces results."[3] The strategy is working. Gore has grown to more than $1 billion in annual sales and the company has been named one of the best companies in the United States at which to work.

The Tiger at Tiger Oil

Compare Gore's leadership style with that of onetime CEO Edward Mike Davis at Tiger Oil Company in Houston. A memo he once sent to his employees pulls few punches in crisply describing how the boss intends to run things. Among the "rules" in the memo:

1. In case anyone does not know who owns Tiger Oil Co. or Tiger Drilling Co., Inc., it is me—Edward Mike Davis. Do not let anyone think they are the owner but me.

2. We do not pay starvation wages, and there are some people in this world who want to work. I am not fond of hippies, longhairs, sex fiends, or alcoholics. I suggest each and every person in a supervisory category (from driller up to me) eliminate these people.

3. Any driver or employee who ruins a piece of equipment due to negligence or abuse will be terminated immediately by his boss. And if the boss doesn't do this, then the boss will be terminated by Mike Davis.

4. The supervision of you will be more strict now than ever. If you do not want to work for me, pick up your check now, or work under my conditions.

5. Don't take advantage of me because I am going to be looking down your throat. You need the job—and I don't![4]

The Tense Environment at Cypress

T. J. Rodgers's style as chief executive of Cypress Semiconductor was less dictatorial, but not by much. *Fortune* magazine reports that Rodgers always took a seat at the corner of the table at meetings "because this maximizes the number of employees in his line of sight. At Cypress this particular chair has come to be known as the turret seat . . . because Rodgers has a habit of swinging around in it as if in a gun turret, pointing at people at random and firing off tough or terribly technical questions. So feared are these meetings that some employees spend hours studying arcane details before showing up. Others arrive at the meeting half an hour early to claim what are known as 'stealth chairs'—the ones farthest from Rodgers on his side of the table and thus most out of his view." Author of the book *No Excuses Management*, Rodgers developed a factory automation and information system he called "killer software" that, among other things, would stop an employee's paycheck if work wasn't completed on time. When a vice president who was late with employee evaluations asked where his paycheck was, Rodgers, with eyes narrowed, replied, "I am prepared to watch you lose your house and your family, for real." Evaluations were done the next day. Regarding his management style, Rodgers—who has a plaque in his office that reads: Be Realistic. Expect the Impossible—admitted that working at Cypress was like "crawling through a muddy battlefield."[5]

Articulator of Democratic Leadership

The leadership styles at Gore, Tiger Oil, and Cypress are representative of two extremes. Few companies provide the amount of employee participation and independence that is found at Gore, and fewer still exercise the kind of control that is found at Tiger Oil and Cypress. In varying degrees, though, both leadership styles have their place and can be appropriate and effective. Earlier, Plato's reservations about a democratic leadership style—one that emphasizes employee participation—were described. But there is another side to this argument. And no one has articulated it better than John Stuart Mill, the English utilitarian philosopher.

Mill, who lived from 1806 to 1873, had a childhood so demanding that it has been compared to the horrors of the Spanish Inquisition. Mill was "subjected to the most dogmatic indoctrination and the most extreme educational 'forcing' ever suffered by a man who afterward attained intellectual independence." At the age of three, instead of being given children's books and toys, he was tutored in Greek by his impatient and bad-tempered father. At eight, he was made to read Greek; and by the time he was eleven, he was translating Latin. By this time, he had also learned ancient and modern history. He read the Greek writings of Thucydides, Homer, Euripides, and Sophocles. He began a course in logic, reading Aristotle and Hobbes. At fourteen, he was sent to France to study chemistry, zoology, and the philosophy of science.

Mill's strenuous childhood and excessive intellectuality caused him to suffer a mental breakdown at age twenty, but he recovered by reading English poetry, a comforting antidote to his arduous youth. Later he served frequently in the British parliament and was an editor of and intermittent contributor to political periodicals. So great were his contributions that he ultimately became known as the "Aristotle of the Victorian Age." At fifty-three, he wrote his essay "On Liberty." Although its purpose was to define the limits of the power of states in interfering with the liberty of individuals, it was the best argument for participative management that has ever been written.

Mill began by arguing that organizations ("society") should not interfere with the rights of the individual (except in the rare case when self-protection is threatened). This concept later became the foundation for participatory management:

> The object of this Essay is to assert one very simple principle, as entitled to govern absolutely the dealings of society with the individual in the way of compulsion and control. . . . That principle is, that the sole end for which mankind are warranted, individually or collectively, in interfering with the liberty of action of any of their number, is self-protection.

When the Organization Inhibits Expression

Throughout "On Liberty," Mill concerned himself with the problem of organizations interfering with the expression of their members' opinions. He dealt first with the possibility that the opinion being suppressed might be true. In this case, he said,

> those who desire to suppress [an opinion] of course deny its truth; but they are not infallible. They have no authority to decide the question for all mankind, and exclude every other person from the means of judging. To refuse a hearing to an opinion, because they are sure

that it is false, is to assume that *their* certainty is the same thing as *absolute* certainty. All silencing of discussion is an assumption of infallibility.

In management, as in politics, silencing discussion suggests an infallibility that does not exist. Managers are anything *but* infallible. And management is far from being "scientific." Barbara Tuchman's observations in *Practicing History*—a discipline as "unscientific" as management—are relevant. "If history were a science," she said, "we should be able to get a grip on her, learn her ways, establish her patterns, know what will happen tomorrow. Why is it we cannot? The answer lies in what I call the Unknowable Variable—namely man. Human beings are always and finally the subject of history. History is the record of human behavior, the most fascinating subject of all, but illogical and so crammed with an unlimited number of variables that it is not susceptible to the scientific method of systematizing."[6] Management, like history, is rife with "Unknowable Variables," and just as unscientific.

The Importance of Debate

Mill described how important it is for the manager to put strongly held opinions to the test of debate and discussion before he or she considers them to be "true":

There is the greatest difference between presuming an opinion to be true, because, with every opportunity for contesting it, it has not been refuted, and assuming its truth for the purpose of not permitting its refutation.

Complete liberty of contradicting and disproving our opinion is the very condition which justifies us in assuming its truth for purposes of action; and on no other terms can a being with human faculties have any rational assurance of being right.

[Man] is capable of rectifying his mistakes, by discussion and experience. Not by experience alone. There must be discussion, to show how experience is to be interpreted. Wrong opinions and practices gradually yield to fact and argument: but facts and arguments, to produce any effect on the mind, must be brought before it. Very few facts are able to tell their own story, without comments to bring out their meaning. . . . No wise man ever acquired his wisdom in any mode but this; nor is it in the nature of human intellect to become wise in any other manner. The steady habit of correcting and completing his own opinion by collating it with those of others, so far from causing doubt and hesitation in carrying it into practice, is the only stable foundation for a just reliance on it.

Even when the opinion is wrong, said Mill, discussion should not be suppressed. Without such challenge and discussion, the true opinion would become nothing more than dogma—something believed on mere faith. In other words, a currently held belief could be made stronger only if managers were willing to allow it to be challenged by other ideas:

However unwillingly a person who has a strong opinion may admit the possibility that his opinion may be false, he ought to be moved by the consideration that however true it may be, if it is not fully, frequently, and fearlessly discussed, it will be held as a dead dogma, not a living truth.

On every subject on which difference of opinion is possible, the truth depends on a balance to be struck between two sets of conflicting reasons. . . . three-fourths of the arguments for every disputed opinion consist in dispelling the appearances which favor some opinion different from it. . . . He who knows only his own side of the case, knows little of that.

Three Cheers for Participative Leadership

Mill suggested that a participative leadership style—one that encourages freedom of opinion and expression—is important for three reasons:

First, if any opinion is compelled to silence, that opinion may, for aught we can certainly know, be true. To deny this is to assume our own infallibility.

Secondly, though the silenced opinion may be in error, it may, and very commonly does, contain a portion of truth. . . . it is only by the collision of adverse opinions that the remainder of the truth has any chance of being supplied.

Thirdly, even if the received opinion be not only true, but the whole truth, unless it is . . . vigorously and earnestly contested, it will, by most of those who receive it, be held in the manner of a prejudice, with little comprehension or feeling of its rational grounds.

In other words, managers who are not willing to listen to opinions that differ from their own—who do not allow their employees to participate in decision making—make the grave mistake of assuming an infallibility that does not exist. And even an opinion that is wrong often contains an element of truth that would not be known unless the opinion were discussed. Unless widely held beliefs are challenged regularly by differing opinions, their value is lost.

The Acid Test at Rigal and 3M

Mill's participative leadership style was tested at General Motors when Alfred P. Sloan decentralized the company into more than thirty divisions in the 1920s. The main effect of Sloan's reorganization was to give greater freedom to managers who for many years had worked in a strictly regimented, top-down hierarchy. The "new" General Motors was able to topple Ford as the number one automaker. GM's task was made easier by the fact that Henry Ford was the most autocratic manager that the industry had ever known.

At Rigel Corp., franchisee of a number of fast-food restaurants, cofounders John Chisholm and Jim Morrissey demonstrated their commitment to participatory management in a unique way. They shared power by alternating the presidency and vice presidency every few years. They also encouraged their employees to be autonomous. When the lease came up for renewal on a restaurant that wasn't making a profit, for example, Morrisey voted to close it. But the regional manager in charge of that restaurant wanted to keep it open. "So, he told me to see what I could do," recalled Frank Musko. Musko renegotiated the lease, worked to turn the restaurant around, and began to show a consistent profit. "At any other company an owner wouldn't give a manager the autonomy to do something like that," said Musko. "It makes me feel like I am not just an employee; I am a real part of the company." In turn, Musko does the same for people working under him: "I share P&L with our managers. I tell them to run their restaurants like they own them." The founders' message that "they want everyone to be successful" obviously has been heard: the company that started with one franchise has reached annual sales of around $60 million and is still growing.[7]

The Minnesota Mining and Manufacturing Co.—3M— and innovation have long been synonymous. Add participative management to that list. 3M executives make it clear that they don't "manage" the hundreds of varied businesses and thousands of employees that make up the company. Instead they "manage an environment"—one that encourages creativity, adaptation, and constant reorganization and redesign as new ideas and products emerge, evolve, or are stumbled upon (as was the case with the company's Post-it notes). This environment includes the rule that researchers are to spend 15 percent of their time working on a pet project of their own. It includes a crash course in risk taking for all new employees that teaches them, among other things, to defy their supervisors: corporate lore is replete with stories of battles won over the opposition of supervisors, such as how CEO L. D. "Desi" DeSimone tried five times to kill the project that became Thinsulate.

Ostensibly, 3M has a pyramid-style organizational chart with the CEO at the top. Under that are executive vice presidents in charge of the company's three sectors, which are neatly divided into groups, which are in turn divided into divisions. But the chart has nothing to do with how 3M operates. (The chart exists for the convenience of analysts, explained one 3Mer.) How 3M really operates is in a chaotic, constantly moving and changing configuration of researchers, manufacturers, and marketers that make up 500 to 1,000 different businesses within the company. Noted *Fortune* magazine: Beneath its orderly, AAA-rated, midwestern exterior, the place is dotty.

Dotty works. The company's more than 3,000 researchers—scattered among central R&D and labs attached to sectors, to businesses, and to specific technologies—are encouraged to go to any business unit in the company to seek funding for a promising idea; if that doesn't work, they can apply for a "Genesis Grant" allocated not by management but by a panel of fellow scientists. On the other end, the commercial potential of an idea is evaluated not just by the sponsoring business but also by a panel of scientists, manufacturing people, and marketers not involved with that business. Often the result is the realization that an idea has potential application in other businesses as well. And this constant sharing of ideas and new developments throughout all of 3M can result in their use in totally unexpected ways. When a scientist in the commercial office-supplies lab was given a last-minute assignment, generated by marketing, to develop a new fly-fishing line for the leisure-time products department (a competitor's product was badly beating 3M's), he consulted a fluorocarbon expert from another part of the company. That expert suggested using a molecule that had been invented for yet another 3M business. The new line, ready for trout season, sold like crazy—and it was developed by a group of people working together across "formal" organizational lines.

A memo written half a century ago by founder William L. McKnight explains the philosophy of this company that has always resisted autocratic management. His words are inscribed on plaques that hang in offices throughout 3M. In part, it reads, "Those men to whom we delegate authority and responsibility, if they are good men, are going to have ideas of their own and are going to want to do their jobs in their own way. . . . These are characteristics we want in men and should be encouraged. . . . Mistakes will be made, but . . . [these] are not so serious in the long run as the mistakes management makes if it is dictatorial."[8]

A manager's leadership style can range from one that provides an environment in which employees are tightly controlled to one in which employees are given as much freedom to participate as possible. Whatever the leadership style chosen by the manager, it will unquestionably affect productivity and job satisfaction as well as the survivability and success of the organization. This is true for every manager, whether CEO or first-level beginner. There is no overwhelming evidence to suggest that one leadership style is better than another. But the most persuasive argument for participative leadership in organizations is the one articulated by John Stuart Mill in "On Liberty."

TWELVE

CHARLES DARWIN

Only the Fittest Survive

Why is it that some organizations flourish while others stagnate and die? What, if anything, explains the rebirth and apparently rosy future of once terminally ill organizations such as Chrysler and Lockheed? Do organizations go through predictable life-cycle stages similar to those of living organisms? A look at three companies that have experienced potentially debilitating crises provides at least partial answers to these nagging questions.

At Colgate-Palmolive, a producer of toothpaste, deodorant, pet food, and soap, overseas sales had long generated most of the company's annual sales revenue. In the United States, the company lagged behind Procter & Gamble and Unilever, but its poor domestic performance was more than offset by foreign sales. Return to shareholders averaged 21 percent annually, and no one seemed to care that the company was, as director David Johnson noted, "always getting its ass kicked in the U.S." That attitude changed when the company experienced a dramatic 12 percent drop in North American sales and 26 percent loss in operating profits in the early 1990s. Noted chairman and CEO Reuben Mark: "We were jolted out of a little bit of complacency."

The company responded to that jolt with a widespread reorganization of Colgate's North American operations. Several inefficient plants were closed; improved communication among departments shortened the time between the placement of an order and its delivery to the customer; long-established but tired products were revamped. That result was a turnover that in just three years increased domestic sales by more than 20 percent and operating profits by an incredible 73 percent. The turnaround was "all the more striking," according to *Fortune* magazine, "because it comes in a mature, slow-growth market overrun with products." Even more impressive, Colgate became the leader in toothpaste sales in the United States for the first time in more than three decades. And that was before its introduction in the United States of its new toothpaste called Total, described as the first "oral pharmaceutical" ever approved by the Food and Drug Administration.

Total, in addition to cleaning teeth, contains Triclosan, a broad-spectrum antibiotic that helps heal gingivitis, a disease that causes gums to bleed from a buildup of plaque and tartar. Treatment of diseases like gingivitis is estimated to cost $40 billion per year worldwide. Colgate-Palmolive, which spent ten years developing the oral phamaceutical, promoted Total as a cheaper "treat-as-you-brush" approach in foreign markets. The product quickly became a moneymaker overseas—with half of its users switching from competitors' toothpastes. Expecting similar results in the United States after receiving FDA approval to market Total, the company instituted a massive product launch in 1998. And with at least three years required to gain FDA approval for a new product, the company's lead in oral pharmaceuticals remains assured for some time.

Mused Johnson, "Sometimes crisis precedes synthesis. It can take terrible defeat to return with determination and spirit. The missing link was always U.S. operations. Colgate could never be whole without returning to strength at home. Now, I think, it has something bigger than ever before." Or, as CEO Mark noted, "We've come roaring back."[1]

Another company that has survived is Eastman Kodak. Complacent executives who took the company's success for granted failed to recognize the threat that competitors such as Fuji Film presented until the company had lost 30 percent of its one-time monopoly in film sales. Kodak's history as a "paternalistic, inward-looking" company also made it slow to react to a changing marketplace or to see the need to change management practices. Despite restructurings, massive reductions in the workforce, and efforts at diversification by moving into pharmaceuticals and consumer health products, the company continued its decline until George Fisher was named CEO in 1993. Fisher set about refocusing the company on its core business, selling off those businesses not related to photography. He pushed the development of new products, including all-digital cameras and Advantax, a camera that enables consumers to have their pictures put on computer discs. He set financial goals that included achieving near perfection in manufacturing quality to increase profits. But his most difficult task was breaking down employees' resistance to change. He especially needed to move the company away from the traditions of a yearly "wage dividend" regardless of the P&L statement, and equal guaranteed raises, and turn it into a performance-based culture.

Employees were asked what they thought a high-performance company should look like. Then a "social contract" was developed which spelled out what was expected from both sides. Employees pledged to understand both the business and Kodak's customers better, to adapt to change, and to give 100 percent of their effort. In return, Kodak committed to a minimum of forty hours of training for each employee, geared to meet his or her development goals. Supervisors were responsible for documenting and reviewing employees' plans; their bonuses were linked to how well employees achieved their objectives. And Fisher met repeatedly with employees to emphasize that in a competitive and continuously changing market, only those who embrace change and learn to adapt are going to survive.[2]

Colgate-Palmolive and Eastman Kodak are unalloyed success stories; these dynamic organizations took notice of their rapidly changing environments and quickly adjusted their strategic courses. Other companies have not fared as well.

One such company is Motorola, described by *Fortune* in 1994 as "the company that almost everyone loves to love." But then Motorola, lauded for its success in the analog cellular phone business, forgot to pay attention to what was happening outside the company. In the early 1990s, for example, 85 percent of cellular phones used by subscribers to AT&T wireless service were made by Motorola. Its flip phones, the most advanced at the time, "were in hot demand." But even then, market insiders were predicting that the future of cellular was digital, a message repeated time and again to Motorola executives. Yet, when the company introduced its new StarTAC phone in 1996—at almost the same time that AT&T launched its digital network—it was analog. AT&T was forced to turn to Nokia and Ericsson for digital handsets, and soon less than 40 percent of AT&T wireless cell phones came from Motorola. By 1998, the company's share of the U.S. cellular phone market had plunged from 54 percent to 41 percent. "It is absolutely amazing to me that [Motorola] lost their way," said Maggie Wilderotter, a former top executive with AT&T Wireless Services, who was one of the people urging Motorola to develop a digital phone. "We were very forthcoming with what we wanted."

Failure to develop a digital phone was just one of Motorola's problems. Wholesale distributors complained that the company's attempt to keep its margins high by distributing cell phones through a very limited number of companies made competitive purchasing impossible. Retailers claimed Motorola's phones weren't competitive against Nokia's, with its longer-life battery and built-in games. In addition, the company overextended itself in Asia, adding to its problems at home. In mid-1998, CEO Chris Galvin announced that the company would take a $1.95 billion charge and lay off 15,000 employees. As Motorola stock continued to drop, customers and investors alike ranted at Motorola's seeming inability to adjust to its changing market. Noted one money manager succinctly: "It's not as though people weren't barking and screaming to management about what was going wrong."[3]

What can be learned about the life cycle of organizations from these three examples? Colgate-Palmolive and Eastman Kodak coped successfully with their shifting markets. They adapted. Their willingness to change enabled them not only to survive but to succeed as never before. Motorola, in stark contrast, stuck tenaciously to strategies that—although once workable—were sadly inappropriate to the late 1990s. The company's inability to adapt caused what was once the standard of excellence in the cellular phone business to become one of the worst performers in the industry.

Adaptability's Discoverer

"Adaptability," that surprisingly rare organizational capacity to adjust quickly to new or changed circumstances, is arguably as valuable as positive cash flow. No wonder it is written about so much and discussed so frequently by contemporary business leaders and scholars. But the subject really belongs to Charles Darwin, the nineteenth-century naturalist who originated the theory of evolution by natural selection.

This tall, gray-eyed Englishman seemed badly matched to the task. Poor health—Darwin suffered from chronic nausea and poor eyesight—and a penchant for procrastination plagued him throughout his life. What is more, his scholarship at Edinburgh Medical School was mediocre at best. His father's estimate of his abilities suggested that he was destined for a life of

irresponsible ease as a blasé country gentleman. In a grindingly
critical letter, the well-to-do doctor wrote: "You care for nothing but shooting, dogs, and rat-chasing, and you will be a dis-
grace to yourself and all your family."

But Charles Darwin possessed a genius that would conquer
his infirmities and overwhelmingly disprove his father's bleak
prophecy. That genius enabled him to develop a theory that
did nothing less than explain life itself. It profoundly influenced
science, psychology, sociology, law, theology, philosophy, and
literature. Darwin became the "Newton of biology."

His genius was twofold. First, like all others who succeed,
he did his homework. He was a born detail man, a meticulous
recorder of facts. To him, science was—more than anything
else—observation and classification. Second, he possessed that
indispensable prerequisite of success, near-compulsive persistence. Both elements of his remarkable genius are illustrated in
a letter to a friend. "One day, on tearing off some old bark,"
wrote Darwin, "I saw two rare beetles and seized one in each
hand; then I saw a third and new kind, which I could not bear
to lose, so that I popped the one which I held in my right hand
into my mouth."

Clearly, young Darwin had developed a single-minded
thirst for knowledge. He wasted no time in finding a way to sat-
isfy it. In 1831, fresh out of his university studies and only
twenty-two, Darwin got himself invited aboard HMS *Beagle* for
an extensive cruise, during which part of the coast of South
America would be surveyed and several Pacific islands visited.
The *Beagle's* aristocratic captain, Lieutenant Robert Fitzroy,
at first had serious misgivings about Darwin. A dedicated

phrenologist and physiognomist, he was certain that Darwin's nose showed lack of energy and little motivation. Nonetheless, he somewhat reluctantly signed Darwin on as ship's naturalist.

The Origin of *The Origin*

Darwin's observations on the trip led with agonizing slowness—the Newton of biology was nothing if not thorough—to the publication of a book, ponderously but brilliantly titled *On the Origin of Species by Means of Natural Selection, Or the Preservation of Favored Races in the Struggle for Life*. Its publication in 1859, almost thirty years after the voyage of the *Beagle*, is itself testimony to Darwin's persistence. The publisher, who had on the advice of one of Darwin's influential friends accepted the manuscript sight unseen, was unimpressed when he finally read it. Darwin's theory, he sniffed, was "as absurd as contemplating the union of a poker and a rabbit." Worried that the project would fail, he gave what must have been one of history's worst bits of editorial advice. He urged Darwin to rewrite the book, limiting it to his observations of pigeons. "Everyone," he breezily commented, "is interested in pigeons." Darwin would have none of it, and was quickly proved right. The 1,250 copies of the first printing sold out in one day, and a second impression was immediately ordered.

The Origin of Species is a wonderfully organized book, full of facts and observations, and it handily lays out Darwin's complete argument in the first four chapters. It also overflows with complicated sentences and Byzantine logic, leading even Darwin to observe, "I must be a very bad explainer." Nonetheless, it caused quite a stir. Ashley Montagu, the famed twentieth-century anthropologist, put it well: "Perhaps no book in the whole history of civilization has made so immediate and enduring an impact on the world of thought and action as *The Origin of Species*—with the exception, possibly, of the Bible."

Darwin's theory, like most other great ideas, was not entirely original. Its genesis was his reading of Thomas Malthus's "Essay on Population," in which Malthus contended that populations tended to increase geometrically and food production arithmetically and that only checks such as war, disease, and famine would prevent the extinction of humankind. Darwin simply substituted his theory, the theory of "natural selection," for the natural checks of Malthus.

Darwin's argument was based on three observations and on two inferences drawn from them. From the first two observations—that the numbers of all living things tend to increase geometrically and, in seeming contradiction, that a given species tends to remain fairly constant in number—he inferred that a struggle for existence prevents geometric increase and holds down the numbers of any particular group. From his third observation—that all living things vary—he constructed his second and most famous inference: The fittest survive by a process of natural selection.

These were the building blocks of Darwin's theory of evolution. In the introduction to *The Origin of Species*, Darwin described this process and argued that the ability to adapt is its cornerstone:

As many more individuals of each species are born than can possibly survive; and as, consequently, there is a frequently recurring struggle for existence, it follows that any being, if it vary however slightly in any manner profitable to itself, under the complex and sometimes varying conditions of life, will have a better chance of surviving, and thus be *naturally selected*. . . . From the strong principle of inheritance, any selected variety will tend to propagate its new and modified form.

Organizations and Organisms

What does natural selection have to do with leadership? Do organizations have life cycles similar to those of living organisms? Can we turn Darwin's theory of evolution into a theory of the firm? Is the "biological analogy" applicable to business? Probably. Alfred Marshall, the famous economist, introduced the idea of a "life cycle" for organizations when he likened the growth and decline of business organizations to the stages in a forest's life. This was pure Darwin. And Kenneth Boulding, the father of modern systems theory, has argued that "individual, family, firm, nation, and civilization all follow the same grim law, and the history of any organism is strikingly reminiscent of the rise and fall of populations on the road to extinction."[4]

The Darwinian analogy is of immense relevance to business leaders because it dramatizes the crucial importance of adaptability. Organizations, like living organisms, must adapt in a changing environment if they are to survive. It is as true in the economic system as it is in nature that

> natural selection is daily and hourly scrutinizing, throughout the world, the slightest variations; rejecting

those that are bad, preserving and adding up all that are good; silently and insensibly working, *whenever and wherever opportunity offers*, at the improvement of each organic being.

Darwin showed that the degree of adaptation need not be dramatic; minor adjustments to the environment may well make the difference between survival and extinction. The woodpecker, for example, displays remarkably subtle adaptations to its ecological niche. Like all other birds, it possesses general "birdlike" characteristics. It has feathers, wings, a beak, clawed scaly feet, and so forth. But its adaptation has resulted in some special features. Two toes (instead of the usual one) on each foot are turned backward, enabling it to get a firm hold on the bark of a tree. Its stiff tail feathers prop it in position. Its stout and especially strong beak enables it to chisel a hole through the bark. And its exceptionally long tongue enables it to take insects from the bottom of holes.

Darwinism at Continental

Nature is full of examples of plant and animal species that have succeeded or failed as a result of how well they have adapted to their changing environments. So is business. Colgate-Palmolive adapted to its weakening domestic market niche by reorganizing and emphasizing new products. Eastman Kodak adapted to a changing market and the need for a performance-based culture. Motorola, on the other hand, kept pushing products that didn't meet current demands and got whipped by the competition. It failed to adapt to changing conditions.

One of the most dramatic examples of adaptation is the transformation that has been taking place at Continental Airlines. After a decade of cost cutting that resulted in increasingly unreliable and unpredictable service, fewer passengers, and low employee morale, Gordon Bethune was named president of Continental in 1994. He immediately set out to change the company's culture, an effort that resulted in the company's posting quarter after quarter of record results and a nearly 2,000 percent rise in stock price.

Bethune's strategy for effecting this dramatic change was simple. He looked at what Continental's poor service was costing the airline in extra charges when flights ran late—for food, overnight lodgings, or putting passengers on other airlines. The cost: $5 million a month. Because customer surveys showed that the most important factor determining passenger satisfaction was getting to their destination on time, Bethune decided the first challenge was to increase the percentage of planes that Continental landed on schedule. He realized, however, that simply exhorting jaded employees to adopt that goal wouldn't change things. Instead, following his principle that "what you measure and reward is what you get," he offered every non-management employee other than pilots (who operated under their own union contract) a $65 bonus every month that the airline's on-time percentage put it in the top five nationwide. (He arrived at $65 by computing half of what it cost the airline each month in delays and dividing that figure by the number of nonmanagement employees.) "We were going to save money by spending money," said Bethune.

The first month the program was announced, the company moved from last place to seventh in on-time flights. The following month, 80 percent of the planes landed on time. Continental was in fourth place, and above the industry average. A special $65 check was mailed to each employee. They noticed. The next month, the airline had the highest percentage of flights on time of any airline—a first in Continental's history.

Employees achieved the first goal so often that the company raised the stakes for 1995: $100 per employee every month the airline was third or higher in on-time landings. But the reward program received so much publicity that other airlines began focusing on increasing their on-time percentages as well. "So, we adjusted," said Bethune. The company decided that landing the planes on time 80 percent of the time was good work that should be rewarded. "Getting the planes in on time became a central part of Continental's culture," noted Bethune. Perhaps even more important, the culture of "backbiting, mistrust, fear, and loathing" that had developed from years of poor management also changed. "We were getting things done together—as a team," said Bethune. And that feeling of teamwork prevailed, even when management, realizing that the push to get planes out of the gate on time had increased the number of lost bags, told employees that on-time flights "without bags, without people, or with dirty planes" wasn't sufficient. "On time meant the whole system was working on time, not just part of it," said Bethune. Employees responded so well that Continental regularly placed in the top three airlines in baggage handling.

Rewarding employees for working together to run a better airline was just the beginning. The extant employee manual, authoritarian to the core, gave employees no leeway in solving problems; no matter what they did, it was probably forbidden.

It was a culture that clearly squelched any desire to serve customers' needs. The company's new "guidelines" helped employees solve problems by giving them the flexibility to use their resources and make independent decisions. "Do what's best for the customer—and the airline" became the new creed. And when employees were given the ability, as well as the responsibility, to solve problems, they did—creatively and courteously.

Bethune's management philosophy that enabled Continental to adapt to its customers' needs is really quite simple. Give employees goals instead of rules—and rewards if they make the goals, rather than punishment if they miss them. Second, make it easy for people to understand what their jobs are by breaking them down into steps that get the job done. The goals at Continental: get the planes to their destinations in a clean, safe, and reliable manner, with their baggage. "That's it—that's the job," said Bethune. "Now that management is out of their way, the employees do it every day."[5]

Adaptations that give certain organisms a competitive edge within their environment survive and flourish. The same is true for organizations. Those that do not adapt soon die out. But others flourish despite chaotic environmental changes because—like Continental—they encourage creative and innovative thinking, continually seek to improve what is there, and develop new ways of doing business. In other words, they survive.

THIRTEEN

THOREAU

Simplify, Simplify

The merger wave of the late 1990s is the latest of several merger sea changes in this century. The focus of the previous wave, in the 1960s and 1970s, was for companies to expand by merging disparate businesses that had little to do with one another. Leading the frenzy were men whose names have come to define the era. Charles Bluhdorn, known to Wall Street analysts as "the Mad Austrian," created Gulf+Western, which comprised more than 100 enterprises manufacturing everything from cigars to movies. Harold Geneen created International Telephone and Telegraph, the world's largest conglomerate, by buying 275 companies in less than twenty years. Known as the "Geneen Machine," ITT owned everything from Hostess Twinkies to the Sheraton hotel chain.

But many companies, particularly those that ventured into industries they knew little about, soon regretted their wildly expansionist strategies. The great majority of the mergers were disastrous in terms of what really counts: economic benefits to stockholders. Bigger did not necessarily mean better. By 1980, "conglomerizing," once the mark of a robust and healthy enterprise, had lost much of its luster. Corporations, including ITT and Gulf+Western, began divesting companies with the same eagerness with which they had once acquired them.

Enter the 1990s, with the focus of merger mania more often the joining of firms within the same or similar industries to create giants in that industry—sometimes on an international scale. In the banking industry, for example, mergers included Wells Fargo with First City Bancorp, First Chicago Corp. with NBD Bancorp, Bankers Trust with Deutsche Bank of Germany, and Citicorp with Travelers, a financial-services group. In the pharmaceutical industry, mergers included Upjohn with Sweden's Pharmacia AB, and Ciba-Geigy AB and Sandoz AB. Railroad giants were created by the merging of Burlington Northern with Santa Fe Corp., and Union Pacific with Southern Pacific. In the telecommunications industry, mergers included SBC with Ameritech, AT&T with local carrier Teleport, Britain's Telecom with MCI, and regional phone companies Bell Atlantic and Nynex. Entertainment industry mergers included Walt Disney Co. with Capital Cities/ABC Inc. And mergers in other industries included Chrysler and German automaker Daimler Benz; accounting firms Price Waterhouse and Coopers & Lybrand; and Internet service providers AOL and Netscape.

Successful, for Some . . . but Not for All

For some of these companies, just as in the last merger wave, the joining of forces will be successful. Two firms might, under certain conditions, achieve a competitive advantage from merging—reaping scale economies, gaining access to new technologies or global markets, increasing productivity. Yet, the theory behind the value of industry concentration—synergy (that hugely optimistic calculus in which 2 + 2 = 5)—may be as flawed this time around as it was during the era of conglomerate expansion. As the *New York Times* noted, most of the hard evidence from past mergers, along with the anecdotal evidence from present-day mergers, suggests that mergers "are too often the progeny of executive megalomania and deal makers' dreams of year-end bonuses."[1]

The proclaimed benefits of mergers—cost savings, improved customer service, increase in market share, greater return to stockholders—simply do not happen the majority of the time. A survey of more than 300 big mergers between 1987 and 1997, for example, found that in the three years following the mergers, 57 percent of the merged firms lagged behind their industries in total returns to stockholders. Long term, even more of the merged firms fell behind.[2] Likewise, a survey by Dennis Mueller, an economist at the University of Vienna, found that while acquiring companies "typically had better-than-average returns on capital" before a merger, their return afterward was worse than average.[3]

As for cost cutting, the evidence shows that doesn't necessarily happen either. Consider the banking industry, where the

rash of bank mergers was carried out primarily in the name of
cost cutting. When Anthony Santomero of the Wharton School
looked at the effect of bank mergers on costs, he found that in
general, merged banks cut costs more slowly than did other
banks.[4] Increased market share? Noted *The Economist* regarding
drug mergers and acquisitions: Not a single one increased the
combined market share of the companies involved.[5] And anecdotal evidence suggests that improved customer service hasn't
fared any better. When Wells Fargo bought First Interstate in
1996, records were lost and customers had to endure long lines;
as a result, tens of thousands of account holders took their business elsewhere. Likewise, more than two years after the merger
of Union Pacific and Southern Pacific railroads, customers who
hadn't already taken their business elsewhere were still waiting
for the improved service that the merger was supposed to
provide.[6]

Given the evidence to date, it's quite possible that the cou-
pling of companies engaged in related businesses in the 1990s
will prove no more productive than the last wave of merger
mania. That wave ultimately saw the urge to merge replaced
by the resolve to dissolve. It was the start of a corporate imperative: *simplify*. That meant refocusing the company on its core
business. It required a disciplined process of slimming down
while at the same time determining and growing the organization's real strengths. It often entailed a return to paying attention to a company's most important asset—its employees—as
well as its bottom line. But as corporate earnings set new
records in the 1990s, it appeared that the imperative to simplify
became the imperative to buy. As the *New York Times* observed,

highly profitable companies, it seemed—and the boss's ego—couldn't resist the urge to buy other companies with their accumulated cash.[7]

It's impossible to predict how the latest run of mega-mergers will end. But analysts' doubts that huge mergers between same-industry companies will increase productivity make it almost certain that the end will come, marking another return to the corporate imperative to *simplify*.

The Art of Simplifying

Henry David Thoreau, the nineteenth-century American author and student of nature and humanity, understood the value of simplification. His famous essay "Walden, Or, Life in the Woods" is an unalloyed celebration of the art of simplifying—the story of a man who went into the woods to, as he put it, "live deliberately, to confront only the essential facts of life, and see if I could not learn what it had to teach, and not, when I came to die, discover that I had not lived."

Thoreau was born in 1817, the son of a Concord, Massachusetts, pencil manufacturer. Upon graduating from Harvard, he began a career as a teacher in the Concord grammar school. The job was to last only a few weeks. Ordered by his superiors to apply corporal punishment to errant students, Thoreau balked, then quickly resigned, claiming that he could not tolerate such outside interference. With his brother, John, he opened a private school in his home where a more progressive approach to education soon attracted the children of Concord's best families. But this career, too, was to be short-lived, for John died tragically of lockjaw within two years, and Thoreau—who revered him—developed a case of sympathetic, but still near-fatal, lockjaw. In desperation, he gave up the school and joined the family pencil business. But Thoreau was destined to be a poet of nature, not a schoolteacher or a producer of pencils. He soon came under the influence of Ralph Waldo Emerson, who in 1845 gave him "squatter's rights" to some land on Walden Pond. Thoreau cleared some land and built a small cabin, and on July 4, his personal "independence day," he moved in. He stayed for two years, at the end of which time he finished his famous essay.

Thoreau's reputation among his twenty-first-century read-ers as a conservationist, naturalist, and social dropout is in marked contrast to the impression that his Concord acquain-tances must have had of him. To them, he was—ironically—the "man who burnt the woods." It happened in 1844. Thoreau had spent a day fishing in the woods with a friend. The fire they built got out of control. Thoreau ran to town for help, but then—realizing that nothing could be done—sat down on the top of a nearby hill and calmly watched the conflagration. The citizens of Concord were understandably outraged, and Thoreau nearly went to jail for his carelessness. As for his rep-utation as a recluse, two things must be said. First, Thoreau's cabin at Walden was only two miles from Concord and less than twenty miles from Boston, the cosmopolitan center of nineteenth-century America. The fact that Thoreau went to town almost daily and that he frequently entertained guests in his cabin belies the myth that he was an escapist. Second, Thoreau was a successful, if reluctant, businessman, having participated fully in the family pencil business, where he was something of a production and R&D expert. Few contemporary students of Thoreau know that he developed a pencil that was reported to have been better than any other produced in this country.

Like most of the other authors of the great classics, Thoreau was a doer as well as a thinker. His ideas were based on experience—the two years, two months, and two days that he spent at Walden Pond. Although Thoreau was part of a literary and philosophical movement that asserted that spirit transcended matter, he was no idle dreamer. What he discovered at Walden became the raw material of one of the best pieces of American literature ever written.

Quietly Desperate

"Walden" was very nearly not published. Thoreau's first book, a sort of wilderness journal entitled *A Week on the Concord and Merrimack Rivers*, had been a dismal failure, selling only 200 copies. The publisher—whom Thoreau had paid to print the book—unceremoniously dumped the unsold copies on Thoreau's doorstep. "Walden" fared little better, taking more than five years to sell 2,000 copies. In fact, it was virtually neglected during Thoreau's lifetime. Perhaps this was because it was not a book for everyone, but rather was directed only to those who led—as Thoreau put it—lives of "quiet desperation":

> I do not speak to those who are well employed, in whatever circumstance, and they know whether they are well

employed or not; but mainly to the mass of men who are discontented, and idly complaining of the hardness of their lot or of the times, when they might improve them.

In the twentieth century, however, there were apparently many who were quietly desperate. "Walden" gained a mass-market appeal, and it ultimately became enormously popular.

"Walden," like all of Thoreau's other writings, is colored by his distrust of large organizations and by his conviction that they would ultimately overwhelm the individual. Thoreau believed that individuals must never abdicate their responsibility for moral action to the organization. Like Sophocles' Antigone, he was convinced that if the laws of the state conflicted with higher laws of conscience, the individual was duty bound to obey the higher law. In his essay "Civil Disobedience," Thoreau formulated what he felt is the proper relationship between individual and organization. The view he expressed applies to any kind of organization—to corporations as well as states:

> There will never be a really free and enlightened state, until the state comes to recognize the individual as a higher and independent power.

And after visiting a Concord factory that specialized in the manufacture of pails, Thoreau wrote in his journal:

> You come away from the great factory saddened, as if the chief end of man were to make pails; but in the case

of the countryman who makes a few by hand, on rainy days, the relative importance of human life and of pails is preserved, and you come away thinking of the simple and helpful life of the man.

But, more than anything else, Thoreau's "Walden" is a handbook for the simplification of life, for both individuals and organizations, and his most important advice is directed toward those who have allowed their lives—or their organizations—to become overly complex. For them, Thoreau has but one recommendation: simplify. He wrote:

> Our life is frittered away by detail. An honest man has hardly need to count more than his ten fingers, or in extreme cases he may add his ten toes, and lump the rest. Simplicity, simplicity, simplicity! I say, let your affairs be as two or three, and not a hundred or a thousand; instead of a million count half a dozen, and keep your accounts on your thumbnail.
>
> In the midst of this chopping sea of civilized life, such are the clouds and storms and quicksands and thousand-and-one items to be allowed for, that a man has to live, if he would not founder and go to the bottom and not make his port at all, by dead reckoning, and he must be a great calculator indeed who succeeds.
>
> Simplify, simplify.
>
> Instead of three meals a day, if it be necessary eat but one; instead of a hundred dishes, five; and reduce other things in proportion. Our life is like a German Confederacy, made up of petty states, with its boundary

forever fluctuating, so that even a German cannot tell you how it is bounded at any moment.

The nation itself [read: organization], with all its so-called internal improvements, which, by the way, are all external and superficial, is just such an unwieldy and overgrown establishment, cluttered with furniture and tripped up by its own traps, ruined by luxury and heedless expense, by want of calculation and a worthy aim, as the million households in the land; and the only cure for it, as for them, is in a rigid economy, a stern and more than Spartan simplicity of life and elevation of purpose.

It lives too fast.

Slimming Down

Thoreau's theory that people would do better if they simplified their lives has been confirmed time and time again in organizational settings. There is convincing evidence, for example, that complex, multimarket conglomerates do not provide the economic value that they were once believed to provide. Widely diversified companies often show lower capital productivity than that of their more focused counterparts. Such conglomerates as ITT, Norton Simon, FMC, and Bendix have fared less well than the typical Fortune 500 company on the all-important measures of return on equity and return on assets. Too, operations spun off from slimming down conglomerates tend to do better under their new, more tightly focused owners. Their buyers, evidently, are practicing what Thoreau preached. They simplify the enterprises. They cut out fat, squeeze inventories and receivables, and adopt more aggressive strategies. The conglomerates, in contrast, tend to complicate things by adding unproductive layers of conservative management.

The experts call corporate slimming down "optimum utilization of resources." Thoreau would have called it common sense and smart management. And for those managers who fear bucking the merger-and-acquisition tide, Thoreau wrote these unforgettable—and wholly contrarian—lines:

> If a man does not keep pace with his companions, perhaps it is because he hears a different drummer. Let him step to the music which he hears, however measured or far away.

FOURTEEN

ARTHUR MILLER

Death of the Sales Force

In most businesses, the real heroes are the salespeople. Serving permanently in the front lines, their jobs defined by cramped airplane seats, shabby hotels, interminable waiting, and an inexplicable capacity to see a yes in every curt no, salespeople are the firm's trench-fighters, its only link with the cold, cruel outside world. They are the catalysts, the optimists, the unbridled and even quixotic enthusiasts and visionaries who drive the entire organization. Cogent is the simple observation that "nothing happens until a sale is made."

Those Old Sales Heroes at IBM

Nowhere was the cult of salesperson-as-hero more thoroughly the culture of the organization than at IBM back in the heady days before clones and Microsoft. There, under the near-mythic leadership of F. G. "Buck" Rodgers, its marvelously named marketing sachem, the computer giant transformed the once-drab world of selling into the most exciting—and rewarding—job in the entire corporation. IBM salespeople were paid more, and treated better, than anyone else in the organization. IBM's sales organization became the aerie of the 1960s and 1970s corporate hero, and Rodgers, until he retired in 1984, was its high priest. It's an old story, but it bears repeating.

Quite literally the firm's "chief hero," Rodgers stood ramrod-straight, dressed impeccably, played scratch golf and excellent tennis, and jogged regularly. Possessing a remarkable capacity for turning on the troops, articulating the IBM culture, and providing a larger-than-life exemplar, Rodgers was the quintessence of the supersuccessful IBM salesperson. The authors of *In Search of Excellence* captured the Rodgers mystique: "When you listen to Buck Rodgers speak, there's a feeling of déjà vu and you suddenly realize you are listening to the modern incarnation of [IBM founder] Watson."[1]

Rodgers exalted IBM's salespeople by doing one very simple thing: he treated them like heroes. In return, he got fanatic devotion. In *The IBM Way*, a lavish panegyric to his former employer, he gives away a bit of the IBM magic. "Every company," he wrote, "should make it known that the salesperson is a VIP. That is how he or she is treated at IBM. It's not unusual for a small group of the top salespeople to be invited to the home office for informal meetings, a private lunch or dinner meeting with top management, and a friendly chat with the chairman of the board. It's such a natural thing for IBM to do, but other companies simply don't think in these terms. Praise and recognition are fundamental at IBM, but I must admit that an extra effort is devoted to recognizing exceptional performance in the marketing arena. Some salespeople reach star or celebrity status not only in the company but in the industry— and they deserve it. Let's face it—the salesperson is the *source* in business."[2]

How did Rodgers, the quintessential marketing hero, turn those hoary IBM marketing representatives into heroes? One senses by his answer that he was, first and foremost, an entirely pragmatic executive: "Number one, to be a hero at IBM, you have to meet your sales objectives," he says. Nothing very unusual about that. But then you begin to understand the heroic status of IBM salespeople. "Our sales reps are heroes because they're the ones we expect to interpret the customer's needs. Nothing happens until somebody sells something. We pay our marketing people more than anybody else in IBM. After all, they're at risk. They have the ability to make more, but they also have the ability to lose."

That statement became eerily prophetic when IBM's business went south in the 1980s, but IBM leaders in Rodgers's day seemed to possess something guaranteed to make any business succeed: the all-important ability to listen well, not just to customers but also to their marketing reps. Here Rodgers, no fan of mentors, does admit emulating one of his former bosses, L. H. "Red" LaMotte. LaMotte was an IBM executive vice president when Rodgers was a junior "gopher" at headquarters. "He was a great listener," said Rodgers. "He had the ability to sit down with a person and make him or her feel like they were the most important person in the world. And he always praised in public and criticized in private. That's something I've always tried to do, too."

A Career Tragedy

Not many organizations bestow such unstinting praise on their salespeople, and few treat them so well. Perhaps this explains why a pathetic man named Willy Loman, the central character in Arthur Miller's *Death of a Salesman*, has come to be an archetype of the seamy side of selling. Miller's superbly crafted play teaches some rich—and troubling—lessons about the nature, motives, and psyche of that twentieth-century hero, the salesperson. It is must reading for anyone who leads a selling organization.

Death of a Salesman is a play that Miller was destined to write. As a boy, he worked for his father, a successful New York garment manufacturer. Abhorring the way buyers treated the company's aging salesmen, he made this the subject of "In Memoriam," the first story he wrote. Throughout his career, Miller has believed that common men—the Willy Lomans of the world—are as capable of heroism and tragedy as any Sophoclean warrior or Shakespearean king. "I believe," he wrote, "that the common man is as apt a subject for tragedy in its highest sense as kings were. Insistence upon the rank of the tragic hero, on the so-called nobility of his character, is really but a clinging to the outward forms of tragedy. If rank and nobility of character were indispensable, then it would follow that the problems of those with rank were the particular problems of tragedy. But surely the right of one monarch to capture the domain from another no longer raises our passions, nor are our concepts of justice what they were to the mind of an Elizabethan king."[3]

And like Sophocles and Shakespeare, Miller masterfully scrutinizes his characters' psyches. In fact, one of the things that makes *Death of a Salesman* so fascinating is that much of the action takes place in Willy Loman's head. (Miller first titled the play *The Inside of His Head.*) But in a larger sense, Miller is writing about the common psyche of industrial man: his blatant optimism, his preoccupation with success and money, his near-fanatical desire to "fit in," and his frenzied attempts to establish an identity while at the same time joining forces with the anonymous efficiency machine that is his age. "Willy Loman," Miller wrote, "was the kind of guy you see muttering to himself on a subway, decently dressed on his way home or to the office, perfectly integrated with his surroundings excepting that unlike other people he can no longer restrain the power of his experience from disrupting the superficial sociality of his behavior."[4]

Death of a Salesman was first produced in 1949, and it was an immediate smash success. The play ran a total of 742 performances, garnered enthusiastic critical acclaim, and won Miller the coveted Pulitzer and other important drama prizes. It opens as Willy Loman, an aging and defeated salesman, inexplicably returns home after leaving just that morning on a weeklong New England sales trip. Watching her weary husband haul in his sample cases, his wife knows that Willy is nearing a physical—and emotional—breakdown. They agree that Willy should ask his boss for an easier job in the New York office, one that would require less traveling. Exhausted and demoralized, Willy is nonetheless cheered by the fact that his two sons, Biff and Happy, have come to visit. Biff, Willy's favorite, achieved local fame as a high school football player. Returning home fourteen years later, he has become a derelict unable to keep a job.

Willy's life begins to unfold before him. Remembering that he almost joined his brother's successful business, he reminisces about a salesman he met who changed his life:

> And I was almost decided to go, when I met a salesman in the Parker House. His name was Dave Singleman. And he was eighty-four years old, and he'd drummed merchandise in thirty-one states. And old Dave, he'd go up to his room, y'understand, put on his green velvet slippers—I'll never forget—and pick up his phone and call the buyers, and without ever leaving his room, at the age of eighty-four, he made his living. And when I saw that, I realized that selling was the greatest career a man could want. 'Cause what could be more satisfying than to be able to go, at the age of eighty-four, into twenty or thirty different cities, and pick up a phone, and be remembered and loved and helped by so many different people? Do you know? When he died—and by the way he died the death of a salesman, in his green velvet slippers in the smoker of the New York, New Haven and Hartford, going into Boston—when he died, hundreds of salesmen and buyers were at his funeral. Things were sad on a lotta trains for months after that. In those days

there was personality in it. . . . There was respect, and comradeship, and gratitude in it. Today, it's all cut and dried, and there's no chance for bringing friendship to bear—or personality. You see what I mean?

Willy wonders what has become of his dreams for himself and for his family. Where did he go wrong? He flashes back to more pleasant times when his sons idolized him and he was known as a top salesman. Perhaps he should have gone into business with his brother. When a friend tells him that Biff has been stealing lumber, he ridicules him, claiming that Biff is only showing initiative. He learns that his company has taken him off salary and will pay him only on a commission basis. Desperately offering to work for less, he asks to be reassigned to New York City. His coldly unconcerned boss tells him he is no longer of any use to the company and fires him. Mortified by this latest humiliation, Willy decides to commit suicide in order to prove his worth and leave a $20,000 insurance payment to his family:

I see it like a diamond, shining in the dark, hard and rough, that I can pick up and touch in my hand. Not like—like an appointment! This would not be another damned-fool appointment . . . and it changes all the aspects. Because [Biff] thinks I'm nothing, see, and so he spites me. But the funeral—Ben, that funeral will be massive! They'll come from Maine, Massachusetts, Vermont, New Hampshire! All the old-timers with the strange license plates—that boy will be

thunderstruck . . . because he never realized—I am
known! Rhode Island, New York, New Jersey—I am
known . . . and he'll see it with his eyes once and for all.
He'll see what I am.

"It Comes with the Territory"

At the funeral, Willy's only friend tries to help Biff understand
what his father was:

Nobody dast blame this man. You don't understand:
Willy was a salesman. And for a salesman, there is no
rock bottom to the life. He don't put a bolt to a nut, he
don't tell you the law or give you medicine. He's a man
way out there in the blue, riding on a smile and a
shoeshine. And when they start not smiling back—that's
an earthquake. And then you get yourself a couple of
spots on your hat, and you're finished. Nobody dast
blame this man. A salesman is got to dream, boy. It
comes with the territory.

Arthur Miller has created a stirring commentary on the
practical, hard-nosed realpolitik of twentieth-century business.
He wanted, he said, "to speak commonsensically of social facts
which every businessman knows and talks about but which are
too prosaic to mention. . . . When a man gets old you fire him,
you have to, he can't do the work. To speak and even to celebrate the common sense of businessmen, who love the person-

ality that wins the day but know you've got to have the right goods at the right price, handsome and well spoken as you are."

And, in the person of Willy Loman, Miller has conceived a poignant example of the lonely creative individual—the salesman—caught in the depersonalizing maw of the Industrial Era. Willy is, as Miller wrote in his essay "Morality and Modern Drama," "seeking for a kind of ecstasy in life which the machine civilization deprives people of. He is looking for his selfhood, for his immortal soul, so to speak, and people who don't know the intensity of that quest think he is odd, but a lot of salesmen, in a line of work where ingenuity and individualism are acquired by the nature of the work, have a very intimate understanding of his problem. . . . A salesman is a kind of creative person [who has to] get up in the morning and conceive a plan of attack and use all kinds of ingenuity all day long just like a writer does."[5]

What Went Wrong?

The lesson of all this is, of course, to try to discover what went wrong, why Willy Loman failed. Although many blame a business world that views men as nothing more than income-producing machines, Willy's problems were both more subtle and more genuine. He was a man of limited talents who set unreasonable objectives based on overly high expectations. Instead of relying on real talent, he relied on his "god," personality:

> It's not what you do. . . . It's who you know and the
> smile on your face! It's contacts . . . contacts! The whole

wealth of Alaska passes over the lunch table at the Com-
modore Hotel, and that's the wonder, the wonder of this
country, that a man can end with diamonds here on the
basis of being liked!

No one is better qualified to analyze Willy Loman's bank-
rupt career than one of America's top salesmen, A. Howard
Fuller, longtime president of the Fuller Brush Company. In a
Fortune article, Fuller concluded that Willy's problem was that
he could no longer keep up with the physical and psychological stress that *really* "comes with the territory."[6] Willy was a
self-deluded man who could no longer distinguish between
reality and fiction. And although Willy had the enthusiasm
required of all salesmen, it was based more on mere slogans
than on intelligence. He had, according to Fuller, sold himself
by taking on a personality that destroyed his life and his career.
He had hoped that it would ensure success. But in wearing the
mask of the popular salesman, he gave up his real nature.
Willy's career was ill-chosen and destined to failure from the
start. His real love, we learn, was carpentry and working with
his hands. At the funeral, Biff said:

> There were a lot of nice days. When he'd come home
> from a trip; or on Sundays, making the stoop; finishing
> the cellar; putting on the new porch; when he built the
> extra bathroom; and put up the garage. You know some-
> thing, Charley, there's more of him in that front stoop
> than in all the sales he ever made.

The story of Willy Loman is a tragedy because, as with all great tragedies, the cause of his collapse is entirely within him. He was a craftsman who enjoyed working with wood and cement more than anything else—certainly more than selling. Yet, he allowed the myth of success, the Horatio Alger belief that enterprise and hard work alone guarantee fortune and fame, to deflect him from a career that doubtless would have been more fulfilling. He gamely tried to "fit in," to adapt himself to the pattern of efficiency that is the Industrial Era. He tried to serve the machine, and it killed him. And as John Ruskin, the nineteenth-century English writer and social reformer, suggested almost 100 years earlier, Willy's failure was predictable. "In order that people may be happy in their work," Ruskin said, "these three things are needed: They must be fit for it. They must not do too much of it. And they must have a sense of success in it."

That credo seemed to be part of the IBM magic back in the firm's glory days. When Buck Rodgers was asked how IBM prevented the Willy Loman phenomenon from occurring, he answered in a surprising way: "You've got to recognize that it's going to happen, even at IBM. You know that there are going to be a certain number of people who are going to perform at an exceptional level whether you pay them or not. But not everybody happens to be that way. That's why you have to keep everybody up-to-date. IBM has always increased education/training and communications expenditures faster than the company grows. You have to take responsibility for your people, whether they're "retreads" or not. Every employee at IBM gets forty hours of education each year. Anytime a person is made a first-line manager, they've got to go to school within thirty days. If they become a second-, third-, or fourth-line manager, they must go to school within ninety days. We force people back into the classroom environment. Unlike Willy Loman, we don't let our people become isolated."

That New England Territory

Like all great drama, *Death of a Salesman* struck a responsive chord uncomfortably close to home. Miller received visits from men over sixty, tired pilgrims making one last journey across the country. To a man, they told him that the story of Willy Loman was the story of *their* lives. Soon after *Death of a Salesman* opened, a national sales managers' group complained that the play had caused serious problems with its recruiting efforts. Others were more indignant. "It's not true," said a chamber of commerce executive, "that the *Death of a Salesman* gives a true picture. The professional salesman has . . . a life built upon the foundation stone of attitude, knowledge, integrity, and industry." But perhaps the most succinct response to the play came from a man leaving the theater: "I always said," he uttered, "that New England territory was no damned good."

FIFTEEN

ERNEST HEMINGWAY

Authority Versus Influence

Whether to use authority or influence in directing an organization is a dilemma every leader faces at one time or another. Authority gives a leader power—through the use of rewards and punishments, for example—to force change, to set goals for an organization or standards of performance, and demand that they be met. The problem with authority as a leadership strategy is that it's effective only as far as the chain of command goes, and it works only as long as the rewards and punishments matter to people in that organization. Influence, on the other hand, gives a leader power in a different way. Influence inspires people to follow a leader because they choose to. Because that leader has a vision they believe in, or a goal they can connect with, employees adapt to change, embrace new ideas, and take the initiative in helping the organization reach its goals—because the goals are theirs as well.

An article in *Time* magazine highlights the difference between influence and authority: "To have influence is to gain assent, not just obedience; to attract a following, not just an entourage; to have imitators, not just subordinates." Ideas are the "real coin of influence," noted *Time*. "The ones that rank as influential tend to be simple to grasp, endless in their implications, challenging to accomplish but still within the realm of possibility (for instance: Love thy neighbor)."[1]

Authority can get things done; there's no doubt about that. And sometimes exercising authority is necessary—there may not be time to gain assent, to develop consensus by inspiring others to follow your vision. A leader brought in to save a troubled organization, for example, may be forced to use the power of authority to turn things around quickly; taking time to inspire the troops may not be an option. In general, however, using authority to rule an organization in these times is out of favor. "The military command-and-control model went out with red meat," according to management experts.[2] In its place is the use of influence to make things happen, to get others to "buy into" a leader's goal for the organization by empowering them to make decisions, take action, and share in the responsibility for the direction they and the organization are moving.

Of Foss Industries and Dial Corp.

One company whose leader has directed its development not by authority but by influence is Steve Foss. Foss is founder and sole owner of Foss Industries, which decontaminates and repairs the machines used to fabricate semiconductors and includes among its clients IBM, Intel, Ford Microelectronics, and Rockwell and Sybios Logic.

In 1998, Foss was named Colorado Small Business Administration small-business person of the year. The vice president of a Colorado Springs bank said Foss's unique management style had helped him "achieve employee loyalty, dedication, and maximum productivity." That same year, a "rigid" inspection process by the International Standards Organization verified that the company maintains a consistent level of quality control that exceeds the norm. Achieving and maintaining that level clearly doesn't happen simply because Foss has used his authority as the boss to demand it. It happens because employees have made achieving that level their vision as well. Customers also cite the company for its excellent service and willingness to do whatever it takes to get the job done—and that's no accident, either. Foss doesn't just "encourage" employees to take the initiative in meeting customers' needs; he gives them the authority to do so. Employees conduct the company's day-to-day business without having to get every purchase or detail approved.

Unwittingly, perhaps, Foss's management approach meets the criteria for an "influential" idea as described by *Time*. His approach, Foss said, is essentially the golden rule. Clients and employees are treated the way he wants to be treated. That simple idea has influenced the development of a company in which employees "put out twice as much as the average person is expected to put out," because they "take responsibility for what they are doing." Employees give clients exceptional service and the company exceptional productivity. In turn, Foss gives them much more than the average in employee benefits. For example, the company pays 100 percent of dental and medical premiums for employees and their families; employees are given paid time off to perform voluntary community service; plant facilities include a well-equipped workout room (and twice a week, Foss leads a voluntary five-mile hike for employees on company time!).[3] Benefits are important, to be sure, but generous benefits by themselves do not explain employees' dedication to consistently maintaining the highest standards of quality, service, and productivity. Rather it was Foss's influence—his ability to inspire employees to adopt his standards as their own, and not because they were ordered to—that was the critical factor in the company's success.

Others have not had that luxury, or that style. When Malcolm Jozoff, a twenty-five-year veteran of Procter & Gamble, took over as chief executive of consumer products giant Dial Corp. in 1996, the company had lost money for the second year in a row. Excessive overhead resulted from the fact that 50 percent of the company's products generated a mere 10 percent of total sales. Multiple layers of management added to costs, as did a company jet, and posh headquarters in downtown Phoenix. Jozoff immediately set about cutting costs. He got rid of more than 200 managers, moved headquarters to a less expensive location, and sold off a number of unprofitable product lines. Next he moved to make the company more performance based by freezing the base salary of nonunion employees and increasing the portion of their compensation that came from performance bonuses and stock options. And just in case employees didn't understand that their salaries were tied in with how the company performed, television monitors throughout the building broadcast the price of Dial's stock and that of its competitors.

Jozoff's decisions received negative publicity from local media, "decrying poor morale at the company." Nevertheless, Jozoff understood that drastic moves were necessary to improve Dial's performance, and his moves paid off. Sales per employee increased by more than a third in the first year; by 1998, Dial posted increased earnings of 242 percent in two years.[4] Clearly Jozoff relied less on influence than the authority of his office to make these changes happen.

Different Styles for Different Situations

The difference between the styles of Foss and Jozoff, of course, is not just the difference between using influence and using authority to direct or change an organization. There were also vast differences between the two organizations. Foss's organization was healthy and served a specialized market niche, one in which quality control was absolutely critical. His influence created a company culture in which superior performance and productivity were the employees' norms, not simply the boss's demands. Profits were the result of everyone in the company working toward the same goal.

Whereas Foss faced the task of building an organization in which employees embraced his vision for the company and helped bring it to fruition, Jozoff needed to take charge of a company facing declining share prices, operating deficits, a number of poorly performing product lines, and an inflated managerial staff. The decisions he made to turn things around were not popular, but they worked. Major problems sometimes call for radical solutions—there simply isn't the time to wait for influence to do its work.

Whatever the style, and whether building a new organization or turning around a troubled one, the leader must start not with the "things" of the organization (machines, numbers, or plans) but with the *people*. And not just the people at the top. After all, it's the people involved in the daily routines of customer interaction, production, quality control, cost containment, or any number of other details that really make the difference in an organization. "Obedient" employees, subordinate to those above them, do enough to get by. "Assenting" employees, imitating the actions of those who have influenced them, do whatever it takes to get the job done.

A Novel Approach to Turning an Organization Around

Few classics better demonstrate the difference between the use of influence and authority in leading an organization than Ernest Hemingway's *For Whom the Bell Tolls*. Published in 1940, the book is a product of its author's interest and involvement in the Spanish Civil War. And perhaps no quotation better epitomizes the relationship between the individual and the organization than the one from the seventeenth-century English poet John Donne that appears at the beginning of the book:

> No man is an Iland, intire of it selfe; every man is a peece of the Continent, a part of the maine; if Clod bee washed away by the Sea, Europe is the lesse, as well as if a Promontorie were, as well as if a Mannor of thy friends or of thine owne were; any mans death diminishes me, because I am involved in Mankinde; And therefore never send to know for whom the bell tolls; It tolls for thee.

Hemingway was born in Oak Park, Illinois, in 1899, the son of a successful physician and his musically talented wife. From his father, he inherited a love of the outdoors and an enthusiasm for guns. His mother sought to teach him to play the cello. He started early in his writing career by contributing to and editing his school newspaper. Later, after being rejected by the army because of an eye injury, he became a reporter for the *Kansas City Star*. Seeking more excitement, he enlisted as an ambulance driver on the Italian front in World War I, where he was severely wounded at the age of eighteen. In the 1920s and 1930s, he became part of Gertrude Stein's "lost generation" in Europe, his reputation growing all the while (he wrote *The Sun Also Rises* in 1926 and *A Farewell to Arms* in 1929). When the Spanish Civil War broke out in 1936, he went to Spain as a war correspondent. His experiences there became the raw material of *For Whom the Bell Tolls*.

Like all of Hemingway's other books, *For Whom the Bell Tolls* focuses on man's fate as he faces the difficult problems of living in the Industrial Era. But there is much more of interest in this book. It closely scrutinizes the dramatic human issues of turning around a troubled organization, enabling leaders to understand better the differences between authority and influence. In one episode, Hemingway illustrates how influence can be more effective than the use of authority when working in a tight-knit group. In another, authority is the basis for group action.

Relying on Influence

In the first episode, Hemingway tells the story of Robert Jordan, an American college instructor of Spanish who was fighting as a demolition expert with the Loyalists. Jordan was highly valued as a man who could destroy the lifelines of the Fascists—bridges, roads, and other heavy installations. Assigned the task of destroying a bridge in the mountains northwest of Madrid, he joined a group of Loyalists who knew the mountains and how to fight in them. Jordan knew that he must lead the group in order to achieve his objective. Its current leader, a guerrilla named Pablo, had no intention of relinquishing command. Jordan, in other words, faced the same situation that any new manager must face—whether joining an already established work group or building a new one. He had to gain acceptance before he could exercise leadership.

He did it by using his newness in the group and the curiosity it engendered to draw people toward him. He did it by listening, by not forcing himself on the group. Instead, he let its members displace their leader so that he would not be regarded as a usurper, as may be seen in this dialogue between two of the guerrillas:

"Pablo was brave in the beginning," Anselmo said. "Pablo was something serious in the beginning."

"He killed more people than the cholera," the gypsy said. "At the start of the movement, Pablo killed more people than the typhoid fever."

"But since a long time he is *muy flojo*," Anselmo said. "He is very flaccid. He is very much afraid to die."

"It is possible that it is because he has killed so many at the beginning," the gypsy said philosophically. "Pablo killed more than the bubonic plague."

"That and the riches," Anselmo said. "Also he drinks very much. Now he would like to retire like a *matador de toros*. Like a bullfighter. But he cannot retire."

The actual transfer of leadership did not come easily. At the moment of confrontation, the group fully expected Jordan to kill Pablo, but he declined to do so. Afterward, he silently considered his decision:

It is true, as the gypsy says, that if they expected me to kill Pablo then I should have done that. But it was never clear to me that they did expect that. For a stranger to kill where he must work with the people afterwards is very bad. It may be done in action, and it may be done

if backed by sufficient discipline, but in this case I think
it would be very bad.

Jordan decided that it would be far better to be "invited" to
become the group's leader than to seize power himself. It was a
wise strategy. After all, his mission was to destroy the bridge. He
alone knew how to do that, but he knew little else. He would
have to rely on the guerrillas for knowledge of the surrounding
terrain. He had to rely on them for support. They, too, needed
him. Thus, the developing reliance and trust became mutual.
Jordan participated in reconnaissance raids with the group. He
did so in the role of student, not as the group leader. He was
careful to use his influence only for decisions that directly
related to his goal of destroying the bridge.

Robert Jordan's story provides a view of leadership based
on influence rather than authority. Jordan allowed himself to be
guided and instructed by the guerrillas' knowledge and expertise. He respected each of the guerrillas for what he or she had
to offer. His leadership was much like that of real-life leaders
who discover, often to their amazement, that the way to get
real authority is to start giving it away. And although Foss's job
was to build a new organization rather than lead an existing
one, his experiences were similar. He respected his employees
for their knowledge. He let them use their knowledge and ability to help guide and direct the company. Rather than order
them to give customers the highest possible service, he empow-
ered his employees to give that service—and they did. Power,
after all, does not derive just from an individual's level in the

organizational hierarchy. Social scientists John French and Bertram Raven have discovered five "power sources": reward power (a supervisor's capacity to recompense work well done), coercive power (the ability to punish an errant employee), legitimate power (based on a manager's place in the hierarchy or job description), expert power (doctors and other professionals have it), and referent power (resulting from a subordinate's desire to emulate the boss).[5]

Depending on Authority

In stark contrast to the episode showing Jordan's use of influence is another episode in the novel. A group of Fascist soldiers was attacking the guerrillas and had them surrounded on a hilltop. The guerrillas were being overwhelmed, but they still maintained a commanding position at the crest of the hill. The officer in charge of the Fascists ordered his men to advance; they did, and were promptly shot down. The guerrillas then played dead in order to attract the enemy. The Fascist officer fell for the ruse and ordered one of the enlisted men to walk up to the guerrilla position to make certain that all of the guerrillas were dead. The frightened enlisted man refused, sure of a trap. The officer put a pistol to his back and repeated the order:

> "You don't *want* to?" The captain pushed the pistol against the small of the man's back. "You don't *want* to?"
> "I am afraid, my captain," the soldier said with dignity.

The conversation continued, and although the enlisted man was not shot, he still refused to follow the order. Then the captain ordered a lieutenant to make the walk with him. The lieutenant too, refused:

I hate these pistol brandishers, Berrendo was thinking. They cannot give an order without jerking a gun out. . . .

"I will go if you order me to. But under protest," Lieutenant Berrendo told the captain.

The captain's authority was tied to his pistol and his threats. And it was effective only as long as his threatened punishment had power over the men. Only the lieutenant responded to the captain's authority and obeyed him, though under protest. Finally, the captain, author of his own destiny, walked alone up the hill. The guerrillas killed him.

Contrasting Ways to Lead

For Whom the Bell Tolls scrutinizes two contrasting ways to lead. Robert Jordan drew on the strengths of his people and was successful in accomplishing his goals. The Fascist captain ignored his people and was left alone to carry out his own orders. Jordan allowed his influence, and that of his people, to shape the course of events. The captain relied solely on authority and failed.

Authority and influence are two of the most important tools of the leader. Authority is granted automatically as part of the credentials of the job. It is usually formalized by a written job description that states with great precision who reports to whom, when, and why. Its power depends not on whether people agree with the person in authority, but whether the rewards and punishments are enough to influence their behavior. The power of influence is more elusive. As a leadership strategy, influence requires a willingness to guide—not command—employees. It takes time and patience. It involves the nurturing of an organizational culture in which employees are the initiators of change because they see the need for it. Influence empowers employees and in the process, empowers the organization as well.

Influence belongs to the part of leading that is mostly magic—the classic touch.

NOTES

PART ONE

CHAPTER ONE

1. Peter Passell, "When Mega-Mergers Are Mega-Busts," *New York Times*, May 17, 1998, p. 18; Daniel Machalaba, "Wrong Track: A Big Railroad Merger Goes Terribly Awry in a Very Short Time," *Wall Street Journal*, October 2, 1997, p. A1; Howard S. Abramson, "Union Pacific Merger Was Quick to Derail," *Cleveland Plain Dealer*, August 23, 1998, p. 10H.
2. Abramson, p. 10H.
3. Richard Turner, "Power Failure: Michael Ovitz Was Hollywood's Most High-Voltage Dealmaker," *Newsweek*, December 23, 1996, p. 34; Frank Rose, "What Ever Happened to Michael Ovitz," *Fortune*, July 7, 1997, pp. 120–29.
4. Gail Edmondson, "'Halfway There' at Siemens Nixdorf," *Business Week*, November 18, 1996, p. 178B.
5. William H. Mobley, "Where Have All the Golfers Gone?," *Personnel Journal*, July 1977, p. 339.

6. Fred E. Schuster and Alva F. Kindall, "Management by Objectives: Where We Stand—A Survey of the Fortune 500," *Human Resource Management* 13, no. 1 (Spring 1974), pp. 8–11.

7. Henry Goldblatt, "AT&T Finally Has an Operator," *Fortune*, February 16, 1998, pp. 79+.

CHAPTER TWO

1. Justin Fox, "Merger of Equals? Try *Murder* of Equals," *Fortune*, August 17, 1998, p. 30.

2. Janet Guyon, "A Mangled Merger," *Fortune*, March 30, 1998, p. 32.

3. Robert Frank and Thomas M. Burton, "Side Effects of Cross-Border Merger Results in Headaches for a Drug Company," *Wall Street Journal*, February 4, 1997, p. A1; *The Economist*, February 7, 1998, p. 63.

4. Cindy Krischer Goodman, "Florida Execs Work for Smooth Merger for Price Waterhouse, Coopers & Lybrand," *Miami Herald*, July 6, 1998, p. 13–36.

5. Ram Charan, "Two on Top," *Fortune*, May 25, 1998, pp. 193+.

6. "Corporate Culture Shock: An IBM–Apple Computer Joint Venture," *Fortune*, April 5, 1993, p. 44.

7. Chester I. Barnard, *The Functions of the Executive* (Cambridge, Mass.: Harvard University Press, 1958), pp. 193–4.

8. Jack Falvey, "Disorganized Like a Fox: The Sly Boss," *Wall Street Journal*, September 17, 1984, p. 28.

9. Peter Drucker, *The Effective Executive* (New York: Harper & Row, 1967), p. 114.

10. Allan Cox, *The Making of the Achiever* (New York: Dodd, Mead, 1985).

11. Nancy Ann Jeffrey and Robert Langreth, "Viagra's Lesson: New Drugs, Unknown Risks," *Wall Street Journal*, June 10, 1998, p. B1.

CHAPTER THREE

1. Marc Ballon, "Extreme Managing," *Inc.*, July 1998, pp. 60–72.
2. John A. Byrne, "Jack," *Business Week*, June 8, 1998, p. 90.
3. Peter Drucker, *The Effective Executive* (New York, Harper & Row, 1967), p. 148.

CHAPTER FOUR

1. *Business Week*, January 20, 1986, p. 52.
2. Marriott International, Inc., 1997 Annual Report.
3. Ericsson Data 1997 Annual Report, "Do it: A New Corporate Culture."
4. Marc Ballon, "Extreme Managing," *Inc.*, July 1998, p. 60.

CHAPTER FIVE

1. William J. Broad, "Silence About Shuttle Flaw Attributed to Pitfalls of Pride," *New York Times*, September 30, 1986, p. C1.
2. Holman W. Jenkins Jr., "How to Save McDonald's," *Wall Street Journal*, March 18, 1998, p. A23.
3. Robert D. Hof, Ira Sager, and Linda Himelstein, "The Sad Saga of Silicon Graphics," *Business Week*, August 4, 1997, p. 66.
4. Kenneth Labich, "Why Companies Fail," *Fortune*, November 14, 1994, p. 52.

PART TWO

CHAPTER SIX

1. Harold Geneen, *Managing* (Garden City, N.Y.: Doubleday, 1984).
2. Leona E. Tyler, *Individual Differences: Abilities and Motivational Directions* (New York: Appleton-Century-Crofts, 1974).

3. Ivor Davis, "Boxer Foreman Steps into the Sitcom Ring," *San Francisco Chronicle*, October 24, 1993, p. 41.
4. John Jewkes, David Sawyers, and Richard Stillerman, *The Sources of Invention* (London: Macmillan, 1969), p. 97.

CHAPTER SEVEN

1. Glenn Burkins, "A Special News Report About Life on the Job—and Trends Taking Shape There," *Wall Street Journal*, April 22, 1997, p. A1.
2. Hal Lancaster, "Workday Etiquette: Know the Right Fork and Watch That E-Mail," *Wall Street Journal*, April 21, 1998, p. B1.
3. Ibid.

CHAPTER EIGHT

1. "How to Merge," *The Economist*, January 9, 1999, pp. 21–3.
2. Kenneth Labich, "Why Companies Fail," *Fortune*, November 14, 1994, p. 52.
3. "Why Too Many Mergers Miss the Mark," *The Economist*, January 4, 1997, pp. 57–8.
4. Thomas A. Stewart, "New Ways to Exercise Power," *Fortune*, November 6, 1989, p. 52.
5. John A. Byrne, "Jack," *Business Week*, June 8, 1998, p. 90.
6. Stewart, p. 52.
7. Marilyn Moats Kennedy, *Powerbase: How to Build It/How to Keep It* (New York: Macmillan, 1984).
8. Labich, p. 52.

CHAPTER NINE

1. Harold C. Goddard, *The Meaning of Shakespeare* (Chicago: University of Chicago Press, 1951), p. 1.
2. Ibid., p. 270.

3. Eileen P. Gunn, "AIG: Aggressive. Inscrutable. Greenberg." *Fortune,* April 27, 1998, pp. 106+.

4. John J. Keller, "Outside In: How AT&T Directors Decided It Was Time for Change at the Top," *Wall Street Journal,* October 20, 1997, p. A1.

5. John A. Byrne, Jennifer Reingold, and Richard A. Melcher, "Wanted: A Few Good CEOs," *Business Week,* August 11, 1997, p. 64.

6. Ibid.

7. Brian Dumaine, "America's Toughest Bosses," *Fortune,* October 18, 1993, p.43.

8. Michael Selz, "Small Business (A Special Report): The End Game," *Wall Street Journal,* May 22, 1995, p. R24.

9. Walter Kiechel, "Office Hours," *Fortune,* December 10, 1984, p. 238.

10. Selz, p. 24.

11. Byrne, Reingold, and Melcher, p. 64.

12. Gwen Kinkead, "Family Business Is a Passion Play," *Fortune,* June 30, 1980, p. 70.

13. Pauline Clance, *The Imposter Phenomenon* (Atlanta: Peachtree Publications, 1985).

14. Weston H. Agor, "Using Intuition to Manage Organizations in the Future," *Business Horizons,* July-August 1984, p. 49.

15. Quinn Spitzer and Ron Evans, "The New Business Leader: Socrates with a Baton," *Strategy & Leadership,* September/October 1997, pp. 32–8.

16. Marcia Yudkin, "Are You Intuitive?" *Natural Health,* May-June 1994, p. 70.

17. *Inc.,* October 1986, p. 35.

18. Marshall Loeb, "How to Grow a New Product Every Day (Rubbermaid Corp.)," *Fortune,* November 14, 1994, p. 269.

19. Ralph R. King Jr., "R&D 'Assembly Line' Revs Up Genentech," *Wall Street Journal,* March 12, 1998, p. B1.

20. Roy Rowan, *The Intuitive Manager* (Boston: Little, Brown, 1986).

21. Thomas A. Stewart, "New Ways to Exercise Power," *Fortune,* November 6, 1989, p. 52.

22. G. Wilson Knight, *The Wheel of Fire* (London: Methuen, 1930), p. 140.

23. Goddard, p. 496.

24. Patricia Sellers, "Can Chainsaw Al Really Be a Builder?" *Fortune*, January 12, 1998, p. 118.

25. John A. Byrne, "How Al Dunlap Self-Destructed," *Business Week*, July 6, 1998, pp. 58+.

26. Eric N. Berg, "Accused Executive Study in Contrasts," *New York Times*, May 14, 1986, section 4, p. 1.

27. John Connors, "Analysis, Action, and the Role of the Manager," in *Proceedings of the Hartwick Humanities in Management Institute*, Hartwick College, Oneonta, N.Y., April 1986, p. 10.

28. David C. McClelland and David H. Burnham, "Power Is the Great Motivator," *Harvard Business Review*, March-April 1976, pp. 100–110.

PART THREE

1. Erich Fromm, *The Sane Society* (New York: Reinhardt, 1955), pp. 88–9.

2. David Riesman, *The Lonely Crowd* (New Haven, Conn.: Yale University Press, 1950).

3. John Kenneth Galbraith, *New York Times Book Review*, October 21, 1984, p. 40.

4. Theodore T. Herbert and Ralph W. Estes, *Academy of Management Review*, October 1977, p. 662.

CHAPTER TEN

1. Robert Nisbet, *History of the Idea of Progress* (New York: Basic Books, 1980), p. ix.

2. W. M. Fruin, "The Family as a Firm and the Firm as a Family in Japan: The Case of Kikkoman Shoyu Company," *Journal of Family History* 5 (1980), pp. 432–99; adapted from Barbara S. Lawrence, "Historical Perspective: Using the Past to Study the Present," *Academy of Management Review* 9, no. 2 (1984), pp. 307–12.

3. Rosabeth Moss Kanter, *The Change Masters* (New York: Simon & Schuster, 1983), p. 133.

4. Kenneth Labich, "Why Companies Fail," *Fortune*, November 14, 1994, p. 52.

5. Judith Rehak, "CEO Without an Office," *Chief Executive*, March 1, 1997, p. 25.

6. William A. Schiemann, "Why Change Fails," *Across the Board*, April 1992, p. 53.

7. Labich, p. 52.

8. Gerald F. Seib, "Top General: Vessey of Joint Chiefs Helps Give the Military Clout in White House," *Wall Street Journal*, March 22, 1984, p. 1.

9. John Gardner, *Self-Renewal* (New York: Harper & Row, 1963), p. 6.

10. Judith D. Schwartz, "Look Back to Get Ahead," *Success!*, April 1986, p. 18.

11. Kanter, p. 283.

CHAPTER ELEVEN

1. R. M. Stogdill, *Handbook of Leadership* (New York: Free Press, 1974).

2. Alex Dominguez, "Team Spirit Fosters Empowerment," *Chicago Tribune*, August 2, 1998, p. 5.

3. *Forbes*, May 9, 1983, p. 122.

4. Mike Royko, "The Top Tiger Is Not a Man to Pussyfoot," *Chicago Sun-Times*, May 8, 1986, p. 22.

5. Brian Dumaine, "America's Toughest Bosses," *Fortune*, October 18, 1993, p. 44–5.

6. Barbara Tuchman, *Practicing History* (New York: Alfred A. Knopf, 1981).
7. "Rigel Corp.: Driven by Unique Management Style and an Ability to Adapt," *Nation's Restaurant News*, January 1, 1998, p. 150.
8. Thomas A. Stewart and Melanie Warner, "3M Fights Back," *Fortune*, February 5, 1996, pp. 94+.

CHAPTER TWELVE

1. Linda Grant, "Outmarketing P&G," *Fortune*, January 12, 1998, pp. 150–2.
2. Linda Grant, "Can Fisher Focus Kodak?" *Fortune*, January 13, 1997, pp. 76+.
3. Daniel Roth, "From Poster Boy to Whipping Boy, Burying Motorola," *Fortune*, July 6, 1998, pp. 28–9.
4. K. E. Boulding, *Reconstruction of Economics* (New York: John Wiley & Sons, 1950), p. 38.
5. Gordon Bethune, "From Worst to First," *Fortune*, May 25, 1998, pp. 185–90.

CHAPTER THIRTEEN

1. Peter Passell, "When Mega-Mergers Are Mega-Busts," *New York Times*, May 17, 1998, p. 18.
2. "Why Too Many Mergers Miss the Mark," *The Economist*, January 4, 1997.
3. Passell, p. 18.
4. "How to Merge," *The Economist*, January 9, 1999, p. 22.
5. *The Economist*, February 7, 1998, p. 63.
6. Passell, p. 18.
7. Ibid.

Chapter Fourteen

1. Thomas Peters and Bob Waterman, *In Search of Excellence* (New York: Harper & Row, 1982), p. 160.
2. Buck Rodgers, *The IBM Way* (New York: Harper & Row, 1986), pp. 60–1.
3. Robert A. Martin, ed., *The Theater Essays of Arthur Miller* (New York: Viking Press, 1978), pp. 3, 5.
4. Ibid, p. 138.
5. Helene Wickham Koon, ed., *Twentieth-Century Interpretations of Death of a Salesman* (Englewood Cliffs, N.J.: Prentice-Hall, 1983), p. 198.
6. Ibid.

Chapter Fifteen

1. Richard Lacayo, "You've Read About Who's Influential, But Who Has the Power?" *Time*, June 17, 1996, pp. 80–4.
2. Thomas A. Stewart, "New Ways to Exercise Power," *Fortune*, November 6, 1989, p. 52.
3. Jim Mallory, "Can This Boss Be for Real?" *Denver Post*, April 6, 1998, p. C-01.
4. Seth Lubove, "Cleaning Up," *Forbes*, December 28, 1998, p. 110.
5. John R. P. French and Bertram Raven, "The Bases of Social Power," in *Studies in Social Power*, ed. Dorivin Cartwright (Ann Arbor: University of Michigan Press, 1959), pp. 150–67.

BIBLIOGRAPHY

Amon, Frank. Othello, Macbeth, *and* King Lear: *A Formal Approach*. Washington, D.C.: University Press of America, 1978.

Anderson, W. J., and R. P. Spiers. *The Architecture of Greece and Rome*. London, 1902.

Aristotle. *On the Constitution of Athens*. Trans. E. Poste. London, 1891.

Bradley, Andrew C. *Shakespearean Tragedy*. Cleveland: World Publishing, Meridian Books, 1955.

Brewer, Derek. *Chaucer in His Time*. London: Thomas Nelson & Sons, 1963.

Brown, John Russel, ed. *Focus on* Macbeth. London: Routledge & Kegan Paul, 1982.

Burckhardt, Jacob. *The Civilization of the Renaissance in Italy*. Trans. S. G. C. Middlemore. New York: Harper & Row, 1951.

Burnham, James. *The Machiavellians*. New York: John Day, 1943.

Burrow, J. A. *Essays on Medieval Literature*. Oxford: Clarendon Press, 1984.

Bury, J. B. *A History of Greece to the Death of Alexander the Great*. 3rd ed., rev. New York: Macmillan, 1951.

Buss, Allan R., and Wayne Poley. *Individual Differences: Traits and Factors*. New York: Gardner Press, 1976.

Campbell, Oscar James. "*King Lear*." In *The Living Shakespeare*. New York: Macmillan, 1949.

Castiglione, Baldesar. *The Book of the Courtier*. Trans. Friench Simpson. New York: Frederick Ungar Publishing, 1959.

Cigman, Gloria, ed. *The Wife of Bath's Prologues and Tale and the Clerk's Prologue and Tale from* The Canterbury Tales. New York: Holmes & Meier Publishers, 1975.

Craig, Hardin. "The Ethics of *King Lear*." *Philological Quarterly* 4 (1925), pp. 97–109.

Dean, John W. *Blind Ambition*. New York: Simon & Schuster, 1976.

Derber, Charles. *The Pursuit of Attention*. New York: Oxford University Press, 1979.

Dewey, John. *Individualism Old and New*. New York: Capricorn Books, 1929.

Drucker, Peter F. *The Effective Executive*. New York: Harper & Row, 1966.

——. *Management: Tasks, Responsibilities, and Practices*. New York: Harper & Row, 1973.

——. *The Practice of Management*. New York: Harper & Row, 1954.

Durant, Will. *The Story of Civilization: The Life of Greece*. New York: Simon & Schuster, 1939.

Elbow, Peter. *Oppositions in Chaucer.* Middletown, Conn.: Wesleyan University Press, 1973.

Ferguson, Wallace Klippert. *The Renaissance in Historical Thought.* Boston: Houghton Mifflin, 1948.

Finley, M. *The World of Odysseus.* Cleveland: World Publishing, Meridian Books, 1959.

Foakes, R. A., ed. *The Tragedy of* Macbeth. Indianapolis: Bobbs-Merrill, 1968.

Fonnard, A. *Greek Civilization.* 3 vols. New York: Macmillan, 1957–61.

Frieman, Ruth. *Understanding Shakespeare:* Macbeth. Garden City, N.Y.: Doubleday, 1964.

Gibbon, E. *The Decline and Fall of the Roman Empire.* New York: Everyman Library, 1880.

Goheen, Robert F. *The Imagery of Sophocles'* Antigone. Princeton, N.J.: Princeton University Press, 1951.

Greene, David, and Richmond Lattimore, eds. *Greek Tragedies.* Chicago: University of Chicago Press, Phoenix Books, 1960.

Hanning, Robert W., and David Rosand. *Castiglione: The Ideal and the Real in Renaissance Culture.* New Haven, Conn.: Yale University Press, 1983.

Hazlitt, William. *Characters of Shakespeare's Plays.* London, 1870.

Herodotus. *History.* Trans. G. Rawlinson. London, 1862.

Howard, Donald R. *The Idea of the* Canterbury Tales. Berkeley: University of California Press, 1976.

Hussey, Maurice. *Chaucer's World.* Cambridge: Cambridge University Press, 1967.

Jardin, Anne. *The First Henry Ford: A Study in Personality and Business Leadership.* Cambridge, Mass.: MIT Press, 1970.

Jones, A. H. M. *Athenian Democracy.* New York: Praeger Publishers, 1957.

Jones, Terry. *Chaucer's Knight.* Baton Rouge: Louisiana State University Press, 1980.

Kamerbeek, J. C. *The Plays of Sophocles.* Leiden: E. J. Brill, 1978.

Kirkwood, G. M. *A Study of Sophoclean Drama.* Ithaca, N.Y.: Cornell University Press, 1958.

Kiser, Lisa I. *Telling Classical Tales.* Ithaca, N.Y.: Cornell University Press, 1983.

Knight, G. Wilson. *The Wheel of Fire.* London: Methuen, 1930.

Knight, W. F. Jackson. *Many-Minded Homer.* New York: Barnes and Noble, 1968.

Lawler, Traugott. *The One and the Many in the* Canterbury Tales. Hamden, Conn.: Archon Books, 1980.

McClelland, David C., and David H. Burnham. "Power Is the Great Motivator." *Harvard Business Review,* March-April, 1976, pp. 100–10.

Milligan, Burton A. *Three Renaissance Classics.* New York: Charles Scribner's Sons, 1953.

Mireaux, Emile. *Daily Life in the Time of Homer.* Trans. Iris Sells. New York: Macmillan, 1959.

Molesworth, H. D. *The Golden Age of Princes.* New York: G. P. Putnam's Sons, 1969.

Morley, Felix. *Essays on Individuality.* Indianapolis: Liberty Press, 1977.

Muir, Edwin. "The Politics of *King Lear.*" In *Essays on Literature and Society.* London: Hogarth Press, 1949.

Nelson, Conny, ed. *Homer's* Odyssey: *A Critical Handbook.* Belmont, Calif.: Wadsworth Publishing, 1969.

Nevins, Allan. *Ford: The Times, the Man, the Company.* New York: Charles Scribner's Sons, 1954.

Nicolson, Harold. *Good Behavior.* Garden City, N.Y.: Doubleday, 1969.

O'Brien, Joan V. *Guide to Sophocles'* Antigone. Carbondale, Ill.: Southern Illinois University Press, 1978.

Paul, Henry N. *The Royal Play of* Macbeth. New York: Octagon Books, 1971.

Polybius. *The Histories.* Trans. W. R. Paton. Cambridge, Mass.: Harvard University Press, 1954.

Rae, John B., ed. *Henry Ford.* Englewood Cliffs, N.J.: Prentice-Hall, 1969.

Rebhom, Wayne A. *Courtly Performances.* Detroit: Wayne State University Press, 1978.

Ridley, Florence H., ed. *Approaches to Teaching Chaucer's* Canterbury Tales. New York: Modern Language Association of America, 1980.

Rinehart, Keith. "The Moral Background of *King Lear.*" *University of Kansas Review* 20 (1954), pp. 223–38.

Robertson, D. W., Jr. *A Preface to Chaucer.* Princeton, N.J.: Princeton University Press, 1962.

Robinson, F. N., ed. *The Works of Chaucer.* Boston: Houghton Mifflin, 1957.

Rolfe, William J. *Shakespeare's Tragedy of* Macbeth. New York: American Book, 1903.

Rostovtzeff, M. *The Social and Economic History of the Hellenistic World.* Oxford: Clarendon Press, 1941.

Rowland, Beryl. *Companion to Chaucer Studies*. New York: Oxford University Press, 1968.

Sayles, Leonard R. *Individualism and Big Business*. New York: McGraw-Hill, 1963.

Schlesinger, Joseph A. *Ambition and Politics*. Chicago: Rand McNally, 1966.

Schmidt, A. V. C., ed. *The General Prologue to the* Canterbury Tales *and the Canon's Yeoman's Prologue and Tale*. New York: Holmes & Meier Publishers, 1974.

Semple, E. *The Geography of the Mediterranean Region*. New York: AMS Press, 1931.

Spengler, O. *Decline of the West*. New York: Alfred A. Knopf, 1926.

Sward, Keith. *The Legend of Henry Ford*. New York: Rinehart, 1948.

Thornton, Agathe. *People and Themes in Homer's* Odyssey. London: Methuen, 1970.

Thucydides. *History of the Peloponnesian War*. New York: Everyman Library, 1910.

Traversi, Derek. The Canterbury Tales: *A Reading*. Newark: University of Delaware Press, 1983.

Trimble, Donald E. Othello, Macbeth, *and* Lear: *Lessons About Behavior in Organizations*. Oneonta, N.Y.: Hartwick College, 1985.

Tyler, Leona E. *Individual Differences: Abilities and Motivational Directions*. New York: Appleton-Century-Crofts, 1974.

Villari, P. *Niccolò Machiavelli and His Times*. 1878.

Wace, Alan J. B., and Frank H. Stubbings. *A Companion to Homer*. New York: Macmillan, 1962.

Webster, T. B. L. *An Introduction to Sophocles*. London: Methuen, 1936.

Whitman, Cedric H. *Sophocles: A Study in Heroic Heroism*. Cambridge, Mass.: Harvard University Press, 1966.

Winnington-Ingram, R. P. *Sophocles: An Interpretation*. Cambridge: Cambridge University Press, 1980.

Woodard, Thomas, ed. *Sophocles: A Collection of Critical Essays*. Englewood Cliffs, N. J.: Prentice-Hall, 1966.

Woodhouse, J. R. *Baldesar Castiglione*. Edinburgh: Edinburgh University Press, 1978.

INDEX